IT'S ABOUT
TIME

Renee Bobson

IT'S ABOUT TIME
Copyright © 2022 by Renee Bobson

All rights reserved. No part of this publication may be reproduced, distributed, or transmitted in any form or by any means, including photocopying, recording, or other electronic or mechanical methods, without the prior written permission of the publisher or author, except in the case of brief quotations embodied in critical reviews and certain other noncommercial uses permitted by copyright law.

Although every precaution has been taken to verify the accuracy of the information contained herein, the author and publisher assume no responsibility for any errors or omissions. No liability is assumed for damages that may result from the use of information contained within.

Library of Congress Control Number: 2022904432
ISBN-13:   Paperback: 978-1-64749-687-6
           Epub: 978-1-64749-688-3

Printed in the United States of America

GoTo Publish

GoToPublish LLC
1-888-337-1724
www.gotopublish.com
info@gotopublish.com

CONTENTS

Before the Beginning...v
Chapter 1   The Beginning and Introduction of Baby Renee..1
Chapter 2   It's Time to Move..9
Chapter 3   Goodbye, Mommy and Daddy.........................15
Chapter 4   Renee Starts School..21
Chapter 5   Renee's Other Grandparents.............................29
Chapter 6   Why Does Granpa Only Tuck Renee in at Night?..39
Chapter 7   MLK and Bobby Kennedy Were Killed!............49
Chapter 8   Family Trip Back to Ancestral Roots.................59
Chapter 9   School's in Session...71
Chapter 10 Renee Really Likes the Drum and Bugle Corps, Especially Jerry...79
Chapter 11 Aunt China Gets Married and Divorced...........89
Chapter 12 Renee Confronts Granpa about Nightly Visits..99
Chapter 13 Don't Threaten Renee in School.....................107
Chapter 14 Aunt China Meets Someone Great..................117
Chapter 15 Life Back to Normal.......................................129
Chapter 16 We Must Save Our Money..............................137
Chapter 17 We're in the City for the James Brown Concert!...149

Chapter 18	Why Is Granpa Doing This?	161
Chapter 19	Granpa Was Right: No One Believed Her	169
Chapter 20	Renee's at the Houston Dance	177
Chapter 21	High School Prom Plans?	189
Chapter 22	There's a Halloween Party	197
Chapter 23	Christmas Shopping and Prom Dress Discussions	207
Chapter 24	Larry Is a Big Hit with Renee, the Family, and the Town	219
Chapter 25	Renee Finds Her Prom Gown	229
Chapter 26	Where Was Larry the Parrot? (Not Larry the Boyfriend)	235
Chapter 27	It's Prom Night!	245
Chapter 28	Last Year of High School	257
Chapter 29	Graduation Dance, Last Dance	267
Chapter 30	Is Larry Saying Goodbye?	275
About the Book		281

BEFORE THE BEGINNING

This is a story about an African American girl born in the 1950s who grew up tall, thin, and vivacious, with long, thick coarse hair, broad nose, high cheekbones, big brown eyes, thin lips, and a beautiful smile. Quite a combination, huh? I am Renee Bobson.

My story will begin at my birth and will include my history. What was the saying? "Those who do not learn from history are doomed to repeat it."

The story will be in three parts; perhaps it will be a three-part series.

Part 1 will start on the day I was born, and it will include actions, people, and events, which led to my birth. It will end with my graduation from high school and my enlistment into the US Army at the age of eighteen. There will be a little slapstick, heartbreak, resiliency, and triumph in each part of the story. My life in the Army after what I went through in my childhood and high school? This should be interesting.

Part 2 will be about my time in the Army, my marriage, my children and family. More slapstick? Raising kids in the Army, dealing with family? Not to mention, what on earth is going on with my husband?

Part 3 will be about my divorce, raising kids as a single parent, working, and retiring. Will this lead to more instances of comedy? Of course, it will. How can personal ads, middle-age dating, and raising teenage kids not be funny? In addition, what on earth is going on with my job?

Furthermore, this story will a contain memories of horrible topics such as child molestation, emotional, and physical child abuse, childhood turmoil, peer rejection, and discrimination. This story will contain touching, heartwarming, and hilarious memories from elementary and high school. I will also relay fond, wonderful memories of family and friends. I will detail my perception of historical events—both heartbreaking and triumphant through the eyes of a black female child, teenager, and adult. Sounds like a contradiction, yet sometimes life can be a contradiction.

This is a typical family story that relatives love to recount, however no one wants to talk about in public. It will bring back fond memories for some people and embarrassment for others. I must admit some parts of this story will not summon fond memories; then again you can't have triumph without discomfort and discontent.

A few questions may be answered.

Could a talented fiddle-playing seven-foot field hand in the 1800s who was originally from Ghana have a connection to relatives of a future generation who are tall, hardworking, and musical?

Could a red-haired, green-eyed woman who was an indentured servant from Ireland be the reason future generations would have an insatiable travel lust? Would it explain why they are the color of dark cream or light caramel with thin lips, green eyes, and wavy hair?

Could ancestors who were forced to move from state to state before they could put down roots explain a certain restlessness in future generations?

Did shrewd business sense and a burning desire to learn and achieve come from earlier ancestors who started churches and bought land after emancipation?

Could family doctors in the nineteenth century pass down attributes to family doctors in the twentieth century? Why did people marry and have children before the age of eighteen? Is this a carryover from the nineteenth century?

Let's start the story and find out.

CHAPTER 1
The Beginning and Introduction of Baby Renee

It was the night before Thanksgiving 1957. Joan Bobson was sixteen years old and was nine months pregnant with Renee.

Joan and Reggie were getting ready for bed as the smell of Thanksgiving dinner wafted up to the top floor of Joan's mother-in-law's house. It smelled good but Joan wasn't hungry, she wasn't feeling well. She was feeling bloated, sick and achy. She was hoping she would feel better tomorrow; it would be Thanksgiving morning.

Her husband, Reggie, was rubbing her back, but it wasn't helping. She finally went to sleep after tossing and turning all night. She dreamt of times not so long ago where life was more carefree and easy.

She fell asleep thinking of friends, family, and loved ones she hadn't seen in over a year. She was excited about the new life growing inside of her, but she grieved over the cessation of old relationships. Would her baby be dark like her, or would she/he be light like her father and sisters? Her father said his grandfather came from Ireland and his grandmother came from Delaware. It seems Joan got her dark skin tone from her great-grandmother and her grandmother.

Her father was a preacher, and it seems all or her ancestors were preachers. They started some sort of Methodist church in Delaware. She dreamt about her baby and she dreamt about the past.

Joan thought back to over a year ago when she met Reggie. She was tall and thin with a tiny waist and long legs. She had walnut brown skin and thick, long, black coarse hair which fell on her shoulders. She had big brown, bright eyes and high cheekbones.

She met Reggie at a house party, and they laughed, ate, and danced the night away. It was one of the greatest nights of her life. Reggie was eighteen. She was fifteen.

Joan Bobson was born Joan Boye in 1942. Joan came from a big family; she was one of eight kids. There were four boys and four girls.

Her mother, Mellie, was a beautiful curvy woman with skin the color of Hershey chocolate. She had luxurious hair, a round soulful face, a lovely smile, and a curvy body. Her mother was a mild-mannered housewife, and her father was a slim-built, caramel-colored preacher with hazel eyes. Her parents were very mild-mannered people. They didn't yell or scream, and they encouraged education in their family. Joan loved her family, but she was entranced with Reggie.

Reggie was tall and thin with wiry muscles. He also had maple brown skin. He had a big white smile, brown piercing eyes, and deep dimples on both cheeks. He had a great sense of humor that, along with his good looks, made him quite popular with the young girls in the neighborhood.

Joan and Reggie were enthralled with each other that night, and they noticed they were a good-looking couple. Everybody told them how great they looked together and what a nice couple they made. It was a night of laughter and delight. They were from two good families, and the sky was the limit for them. They thought they were madly in love; they could not keep their hands off one another.

They saw each other every day, and a month later Joan missed her period. She couldn't figure out why; Reggie and she hardly did anything. That time they did anything only lasted a minute. Much to her horror, another month went by and still nothing, so she told her sister and then she told her mother.

She finally went to the doctor and found out she was pregnant. Her mother told her she had no choice; she had to get married. Joan liked Reggie a lot, and now she had to marry Reggie and move into the house where he, his Mom Bea, his Dad Roy, and his Sister China lived. Joan was excited. She thought being married to Reggie and having a baby would be exciting and glamorous. She was excited yet fearful; she didn't really know Reggie's family. His mother seemed strict, but at least she felt comfortable with Reggie's sister China.

Reggie was also worried. It seemed the days of young girls, football, and high school fun were over for him. Joan felt the same dread; the days of boys, dances, and parties were over for her. Now they were married with a baby on the way.

Reggie worked in the grocery store to bring home additional income for his now growing family. New babies cost a lot of money, and he needed to be responsible like his mom and dad. They ended up living with Reggie's family.

Joan thought the Bobson's house was okay. It was much like the house she grew up in Dorsey, Pennsylvania, as a matter of fact she grew up only a couple of blocks away from them. Bea's house had a nice-sized living room with plastic-covered furniture. Everything matched; everything was green. Curtains, couches, chairs, lamps, and carpet were all green. It looked nice although the plastic on the chairs was uncomfortable. The dining room had a nice oak table with matching chairs and a beautiful oak breakfront. The dining room led to a galley kitchen with all the modern conveniences of a kitchen in the 1950s. There was a white gas stove, a nice white refrigerator, and a white porcelain shiny sink. The cabinets and tile were pink.

The house had three bedrooms. Joan and her new husband Reggie were in one. It was a small bedroom with two beds, one dresser, and one closet. It was the former bedroom of Reggie and his brother Roy who was now in the military. China, now Joan's sister-in-law, was in another small bedroom, and Reggie's parents were in the master bedroom. Joan was extremely tired, and she was drifting off to sleep. *Oh, well,* she thought, *the past is the past.* It was time to get to sleep and get ready for Thanksgiving the next day.

It was finally Thursday, November 28. Thanksgiving Day in 1957. Joan still wasn't hungry, but she knew she had to eat. She was about to sit down for Thanksgiving dinner with her husband, Reggie, and his family, but Thanksgiving dinner was not in the cards that day.

Before she could sit, she experienced a horrible pain, and there was suddenly a puddle of water on the floor. If the pain weren't so horrible, she would not have minded an excuse to get out of this house. The walls seemed like they were closing in on her.

For now, it did not matter if she wanted to leave. She couldn't stay because she just could not stand the agony. She could not understand the crushing, debilitating pain. This couldn't be normal.

Bea told her the pain was quite normal. She explained she was in labor; the baby was coming, and she needed to get to the hospital. Joan was only sixteen; Reggie was only nineteen. They were both scared. They were terrified, yet they were excited.

Bea called an ambulance. It was the first time Joan would ride in such a contraption, and as far as she was concerned it was another thing to be afraid of.

The ambulance came quick for a Thanksgiving Day. Joan was afraid to get into the vehicle. It looked strange to her, but she was convinced to get into the vehicle once she saw Reggie was going to ride with her.

The man in the vehicle put a plastic mask on her face; she was later told it was oxygen. The ride to the hospital seemed like it took forever, but she finally arrived and was checked into a room after what seemed like hours. The pain lasted for eight hours and finally a doctor came into the room to tell her it was time to deliver. It seemed like it took forever, but after all the pushing and pain a tiny baby girl was born.

Joan and Reggie named the baby girl Renee Bobson. The baby girl was only six pounds with skin the color of walnuts and big brown eyes. Her hair consisted of big rings of shiny curls, and she had a loud lusty cry.

Joan knew she had to take the baby back to her in-law's house after she was released from the hospital, and she dreaded it. She wondered why Reggie did not dread the house as much as she did. Why did she dread the house? Why did she dread some of the people in the house? She knew the answer, but she did not want to face it just now. She had too much to think about.

Joan and Reggie finally went back to the house with the new baby, and life changed as they knew it. Baby Renee cried constantly, and Joan had to keep dipping diapers into the toilet to wash off the waste. She then had to wash the diapers, and it was a lot of work. She could not imagine her mother or her sisters doing this.

She wished she could speak to them. She did not understand why they didn't talk to her.

She was overwhelmed. It seemed too much for one person to bear. Reggie went to work at the grocery store, and it left Joan at the house alone with the baby. Her sister-in-law China was great, but she was still in school. China was only ten. She would still hang out with friends and have fun until it was time to come home. Joan could not hang out with her friends or even talk to her family. As a matter of fact, her family did not have much to do with her once she became pregnant and married at sixteen.

Once she became pregnant, Joan no longer went to school, and she no longer had much of a social life. Her only interactions were with her new husband and in-laws. She loved the new baby, but sometimes she felt a little resentful. She could not go anywhere or do anything. She felt like her life as she knew it was over.

She was exhausted and sad. Her only bright spot was when Reggie came home from work, but he was always tired and sometimes, when he wasn't tired, he would go out with his friends.

Joan's mother-in-law worked at a factory and she took in laundry. She helped with the baby after work in the evenings and nights, but she did not have a lot of time during the day to help Joan with the baby. Of course, Roy, Bea's husband, did not have time. He worked at a company that built ships, and, in any case, it was not his job to help with the baby.

Even though Bea helped Joan with baby Renee after work she was terrified of Bea. She was very controlling, and she had quite a temper. When she got home from work, she would tell Joan what she was doing wrong with the baby, which was everything, and she would always belittle her. Roy was mild mannered, but he also made Joan nervous. She would never tell anyone why he made her nervous. Some things are best left unsaid. Besides who would believer her?

China was a big help when she was home. She was kind, she always wanted to help, and she treated the baby like a treasured gift. China was the only reason Joan could stand to live in that house for as long as she did.

CHAPTER 2
It's Time to Move

Baby Renee is here now. Mommy's sister Candy will help.

Joan told Reggie they needed to get out of that house. She didn't like it there, and she needed help from her sister to raise the baby. Her sister Candy had not talked to her in a while, but she knew she would help her. They needed to move to an apartment near her Sister. Reggie was quite comfortable living at home with his family, but he agreed to move. They would finally be on their own and he would be the man of his new house. He worked, and the rent cost most of his salary, but his Mom and Dad would help him out until he could get a second part-time job. He couldn't stay in school any longer. He had a family to take care of and feed now.

Reggie and Joan told Bea, Roy, and China they were going to move. Joan told them there was an apartment available in Candy's building. Bea agreed it might be a good idea. Joan would have her sister to talk to and she would have help with the baby. China could walk to the apartment to visit; it was not far from the house and it was near her school. Bea, Roy, and China were sorry to see them go, but they knew it was for the best, the couple needed their own space and Joan would benefit from living near her sister.

Reggie and Joan moved to the apartment, and Candy welcomed them and little Renee. It was a one-bedroom apartment, but it did not seem small to Joan. It was her own place and her sister lived upstairs!

In the apartment, a small walkway led to a little kitchen. Everything was white. There was a small white gas stove, a small white refrigerator, and a small white porcelain sink. Next to the kitchen was a space with a yellow kitchen table and four yellow chairs. The next room was a living room with a brown fabric couch, a chair, and a footrest. There was a lot of space in the living room; they could even fit the white crib in there. The bedroom had two twin beds and a dresser. There was no room for a crib.

Joan was glad the living room was near the bedroom so they could hear the baby in the middle of the night, but one of the best things about the apartment was her Sister Candy who lived right upstairs with her husband Michael Joseph Sr.

Reggie and Joan's apartment building was across the street from the hospital. It was a relief and a big help for Joan to have her sister Candy as an ally. Candy was kind, helpful, smart and great with children, she was also fiercely protective of Joan. There were problems in Joan and Candy's family however the problems did not stop the fierce loyalty between sisters.

Candy was the color of dark cream with green eyes; she had curly black hair and an hourglass figure. Her mother said she looked like her great grandma Martha who was rumored to have been born after emancipation. Joan was darker with coarse hair like her great grandfather. Candy was twenty-four with a husband

and two children of her own. Her two growing boys, Mikey Jr. and Keith, often played with baby Renee.

Candy often wondered why some of her family was light-skinned and some of her family was dark-skinned. She heard stories of her great, great grandmother who was Irish and from a strange country. The older folks in the family often talked about her coming from a country with rolling hills, whatever that meant. She imagined her ancestors in the olden days.

They said her great-great-grandfather came from Africa, a place where beautiful animals roamed free and lived peacefully with the people there. She wanted to visit Ireland and Africa one day.

For now, Joan liked the apartment building she and her sister lived in. It gave them a chance to be together and raise their children together. Joan and Candy smiled often when they watched their children play together.

Renee was crawling; she was not even one year old yet. Mikey and Keith always made her laugh. Candy always left Joan's apartment before Reggie came home from work. Candy's husband and Joan's husband usually got home at around the same time.

When Reggie came home from work, he always picked up Renee for a minute to hug her and ask her how her day was. He would talk to baby Renee like an adult. Joan always thought this was the funniest thing. Both she and Renee used to laugh.

Renee started to notice her surroundings. There was Mama who had a high squeaky voice, Daddy who had a deeper voice, and the apartment which had rooms for her to crawl to and explore. She found out how easy it was to hold onto furniture to walk wherever she wanted to go. Sometimes she could let go of the furniture to walk. The Mama's voice seemed to always stop her from crawling and walking to places she wanted to go. There was the stove with the fire on top, which looked fascinating, but Mama would not let her touch it. The Daddy was not much better. She thought it was fascinating to play in the bathroom in the bowl they called the toilet, but he scooped her up to stop her from exploring her entire world.

Sometimes the Mama and the Daddy's voices would be louder than usual and fill her with dread.

As a matter of fact, lately it seemed their voices were always loud, and even though she was not yet two years old, she was always afraid. She wondered if the yelling was due to something she did.

She remembered the Daddy yelling about soiling her diaper. Maybe they were yelling about that. She didn't want them to yell, but she didn't know how to stop it. She hoped the yelling wasn't about her diaper. She didn't know how to tell if she was going to soil her diaper. It seemed one minute it was not soiled and the next minute it was. Daddy said she knew what she was doing, but she really did not quite get it. She knew she was supposed to go to the potty sometime, but she didn't quite understand when she should go. Could this be the reason the Mama and Daddy were speaking in loud voices? She felt something was wrong, but she could not quite understand what it was.

She was always afraid. She did not know why she was afraid. She just was. Maybe it was because Mama and Daddy always yelled, and she was afraid it was about her. She also noticed Aunt Candy never came around when the Daddy was home. Renee was quite timid, fearful, and hesitant, especially when Mama and Daddy were together. Even at a young age she knew these were not desirous qualities, the Mama and Daddy kept telling her so, but the qualities seemed to be a part of her personality. Maybe one day she would be braver. She was almost two years old. Maybe she would be braver when she was three.

There were good memories. Renee would walk with Mommy, Aunt Candy, and her cousins to the grocery store and Mommy would sometimes give her a lollipop. Her cousins tried to teach her to skip, but she couldn't seem to get the hang of it. She would try to skip and end up falling and rolling over on the ground. They all laughed and jumped and sang songs. Renee loved trips to the grocery store. They were good times. Maybe things were starting to get better.

CHAPTER 3
Goodbye, Mommy and Daddy

Renee is living with Nene, Granpa, and Aunt China now. What's the hairy thing near her bottom at night?

It seemed very strange. Just when it seemed things were starting to get better everything changed. One day Renee was living in the apartment with the Mama and Daddy. There would be daily visits from Aunt Candy and the world was basically the same every day, but now she was at another house. This house was not in a building. It was a row of houses and the rooms were bigger; there was an upstairs and downstairs in one house.

There was no longer a Mama and Daddy; there was a Nene, a Granpa, and an Aunt China. Renee wondered who these people were.

Renee knew these new people were in charge, and she tried to melt into the background and stay out of the way.

Nene Bea had a very loud voice, and Renee did not want her to be angry or yell. She knew it wasn't good when Mama and Daddy yelled. She didn't think yelling was a good thing; maybe that's why she was here in this new house.

It seemed Renee was still timid and afraid, but she was sure she would change once she got older. She still was not three yet. The only bright spot in the day was Aunt China. She found out China was her aunt. China was only ten so Renee thought she was a cousin, but she was an aunt; she was Daddy's sister. Aunt China was smaller than Nene and Granpa, and Renee realized she was smaller because she was still a child.

She would leave every day but then she would come back and scoop her up and hug her and play with her. She almost did not feel scared when she was with Aunt China.

Renee did like the house. She had lots of room to crawl or walk. She could explore from room to room, and she loved it.

Everything in the living room was the color of grass. There was a lot of furniture covered in plastic, but it looked nice.

She really did not get into trouble for touching things. Everything was covered in plastic, and she could explore.

She especially loved exploring the kitchen! She loved the smells that came out of that room. Nene or Bea, as other people called her, always allowed her to taste whatever she wanted.

Nene loved to feed people, even as a baby she liked to share food and goodies. She never knew this, but her mother and grandmother were the same way. Bea's mother and grandmother loved to cook, entertain, and share food. They would showcase the food and all the neighbors knew to go to their houses for weekly feast. There never seemed to be a shortage of food at her grandmother Annie's house, there was never a shortage of food at her mother Robin's house, and there was never a shortage of food at her house. Bea looked like her grandmother Annie who was an indentured servant from Ireland. Bea had dark cream-colored skin not much darker than Annie's cream-colored skin. Bea's mom had darker skin like her grandfather. He was from Ghana and rumor had it he was a slave who was called a field hand. As far back as Bea could remember there was always food even if they made delicacies over left over crops or animal parts. They could always make a delicious meal and have gatherings of friends in family even if it were in a small cabin.

Renee was always allowed to eat; she was never afraid to ask for food. Nene never became upset when you asked for food, it always made her smile. You would think Nene would be fat because she was always cooking and feeding people, but she was small. She was 5'1 with cream-colored skin. She had brown wavy hair. Although she was shapely, she was not big. She had big breast, a small waist and short shapely legs.

She was a loud, vivacious, pretty lady, she was a sought-after friend in Dorsey, she was smart, and she had a great business sense.

Renee was not afraid of Aunt China who was the color of Nene or a darker shade of cream. Aunt China looked like Nene; she also had wavy hair. The only difference is she was smaller because she was ten.

Renee was also not afraid of Uncle Cheeks who was Daddy and Aunt China's brother. He did not live with them. He was married, and he had been in the military. He was loud but fun and jolly. He sometimes brought his daughter Rosy, who was the same age with Renee, with him. Renee loved it when they visited.

Renee was also not afraid of Foxy, the pet dog who looked like a fox. Foxy was friendly and loyal, he followed Renee everywhere and he was fiercely protective.

Of all the things that Renee loved, food was her favorite. They all marveled at how much she ate without gaining a lot of weight. Her big appetite made them all laugh. It seemed food was the one thing that brought the family together.

She also felt quite comfortable with Granpa. He was mild mannered, and he did not have a loud voice. Granpa would leave every day and when he came home. He would watch TV. He did not have much to do with Renee, but he did not yell.

Before she knew it, Renee was three. When people asked her how old she was she would put up three fingers and say, "I'm this many!" Her days were spent playing with Foxy the dog, playing with her doll that had blonde hair and blue eyes, and playing with Aunt China when she came home from school. Aunt China always held her and taught her new exciting words. Renee liked her world, but something was missing. She saw her Daddy every weekend, but she only saw her Mother Joan once a year on a day they called Christmas.

She wondered why she didn't see her mother more or her mother's sister Aunt Candy. She missed seeing them.

Her father would come to Nene's house on the weekend and pick her up from the floor and play with her and then he would sing with his friends and Aunt China.

Renee didn't understand why he didn't stay, but she knew he would always come back. Nene Bea would tell her every week what day to expect a visit from her father. It was strange, Nene would never tell her when to expect a visit from her mother, and she never really mentioned her mother.

Being three was exciting. Renee got to walk outside with Aunt China. They would walk around the block and say hello to all the neighbors; sometimes they would even go to the store to get candy. Renee had her own room with her own bed, Aunt China's room was right next to her room. Aunt China's room was big with closets and drawers and a TV and radio. Renee's room had a bed, a drawer, a closet, and no TV or radio.

On some nights, Nene Bea would let Renee crawl into bed with Nene and Granpa. They would watch TV. Renee loved it, she slept in the middle with Nene on one side and Granpa on the other side. She always felt nice and secure in the bed with Nene and Granpa. She felt like such a big girl; after all she was three years old now!

The only thing that confused Renee is how she always felt something rough and hairy near her panties under the covers. She wondered if it was Foxy the dog, but she didn't see Foxy in the room. She just laid there and wondered what on earth it was. She never said anything because she figured it was Foxy plus sometimes people didn't understand what she was saying. She was three but you probably needed to be four before everyone knew what you were saying.

Before she knew it, Renee was five and Nene and Aunt China started talking about Renee going to school. Renee was terrified of school; she didn't know what it was; she only knew she would be away from home with people she didn't know.

Aunt China told her school would be fun. She assured her she would meet new friends and learn exciting things, but Renee was still terrified. She was still quite timid, she thought she would no longer be timid at five, but it seemed the older she got the more timid she became.

Things did not change at home, Nene still made delicious food. Aunt China still hugged her and played with her after school every day. She would also take Renee outside to play, and she would take her to the store. She still played with Foxy the dog and she still would get to sleep with Nene and Granpa on the weekends when Aunt China was out with friends.

She still could not figure out what the hairy coarse thing was under the covers. She never saw Foxy, and it seemed to be coming from Granpa's side. Could Foxy be jumping on the bed, sniffing her underwear, and then leaving the room? She could never figure it out. She would jump up and try to find him, but he was never there and Nene and Granpa were asleep.

CHAPTER 4
Renee Starts School

Who is JFK? Why was he killed? Does Aunt China know why?

Renee was five years old, and it was time to go to school. Nene and Aunt China said, "You must go to school in September." They said she would be six in November and she needed to be in school. She really did not want to go to school, but they ended up taking her.

It was September 1963, Renee would be six years old in two months, and she had to face it—it was time to go to school.

The first day of school had come, and Nene walked with Renee to the Maple street elementary school building.

The walk was wonderful, the streets were lined with beautiful trees which had green, red, orange and yellow leaves. It was a beautiful breezy day and Renee had on a new dress with a matching jacket.

Nene held her hand the whole time and Renee felt braver.

The elementary school was a big building with huge double doors. There were so many rooms! It looked like there were so many kids in each room. What was she supposed to say to all the kids? What was she supposed to say to the grownup in front of the room? Aunt China and Nene told her the grownup in front of the room was called the teacher. Would the teacher yell at her? Would the kids not like her? How long did she have to stay there? She was told she had to go every day for a long time. Were they serious?

Renee went into one of the rooms and she sat at a desk in the back. The desk was a little chair with a little table. The top of the table lifted, and you could put your pencil, papers, and books in it. When she sat at the desk it seemed like all the kids were staring at her and the teacher started talking about ABCs and words, which, thank goodness, Aunt China had taught her.

The teacher also talked about families and workplaces of Mommies and Daddies. Renee rarely saw her mother, so she couldn't talk about her and she only saw her father every week or so. Her mommy and daddy did not live with her, and she really did not know what their workplaces were. She thought she remember Aunt China talking about Daddy working in a Supermarket and singing in a singing group, but she didn't know how to explain it to the teacher, also it didn't sound like what the other kids' Moms and Dads did for a living.

Renee just stayed in the back of the classroom while the other children talked, she really didn't have much to say.

After the class discussion, it was time to color. The teacher passed out pages from a coloring book to each student and when Renee looked at her page she was thrilled. It was a Christmas tree with ornaments and presents and a mommy, a daddy, and a child beside it. She could color it with beautiful colors and create a nice picture. She always colored with Aunt China; it was one of her favorite pastimes and she was good at it. Maybe this wouldn't be so bad after all.

The teacher made an announcement in the classroom. She said there were crayons in the front of the classroom near her desk and she invited the students to come on up and get some crayons. All the students made a mad dash for the crayons and Renee ended up in the back of the line. Everyone had already picked their crayons. Of course, by the time she got to the crayons the only colors left were black and brown.

She couldn't color the tree, ornaments, or presents black or brown. She couldn't color the mommy, daddy, or child black or brown because none of the other children colored the people black or brown. All the other children colored the people white. She ended up coloring everything black and brown, but of course, she left the people the color of the paper which was white.

Black and brown crayons seemed to happen every time she went to school; she began to dread coloring unless she was coloring at home with Aunt China.

Renee never talked about family except her Aunt China and her Grandma Bea. She never volunteered information about her parents, and the teacher stopped choosing her to answer questions.

 She was always the last to pick out the crayons and all her pictures were black and brown. She started to notice when it was time to go outside for recess none of the children wanted to play with her, she was the weird girl who colored everything black and brown.

She was very shy, and she did stay apart from the other students. She never felt like she fit. Maybe it was because she was skinny, maybe because she was a different color, or maybe because she didn't talk much.

Finally reports went home to Nene. The school told her Renee was not up to standard with the rest of the first graders. They told Nene Renee would need to repeat the first grade. Nene couldn't understand it. At home Renee could read, she could do simple addition and subtraction, and she colored nice pictures. She knew Renee was shy, but she couldn't understand why she was not interacting in school.

It was November 1963, and Renee was still having the same problems in school, but something new happened in class. It was a Friday. Renee was excited because the next day was Saturday and she and Aunt China would go to the five-and-dime to get ice cream. They couldn't stay there and sit at the counter like the other people in the five and dime, but she loved it.

They would get their ice cream and leave the five-and-dime. They would take long walks in the town. Renee was always so excited about the after-school five-and-dime trips. She was daydreaming about ice cream when another teacher came into the room to speak to her teacher and both teachers started to cry. Renee could not imagine what would make the teachers cry.

The teacher announced the President had been killed. Renee wondered who the President was and what the teacher meant when she said he was killed. She couldn't understand why the teachers were so upset. Her class was dismissed early. It was just past lunchtime, and she was already going home. Aunt China was there waiting for her. She had gotten out of school early too, and they walked home.

Aunt China was more quiet than usual on the walk home and she seemed upset. Renee asked her what was wrong, and Aunt China told her the President had been killed.

Renee knew Aunt China would know what "killed" meant. After all Aunt China was fifteen, and she knew everything. Aunt China said it means he died and went to heaven and no one would ever see him again. His family would never see him again and we would never see him again. Renee asked if he had ever been to their house, and Aunt China laughed. She said no but they always saw him on TV, and he said nice things.

The President had died. Renee asked Aunt China how he died, and she was told he was shot and killed. She couldn't understand why anyone would kill the President. Renee finally remembered who the President was. Nene and Granpa always talked about him. They seemed to like him. Renee remembers them talking about how he was a nice young man who wanted everyone to be treated equally and how he helped put men on the moon. He even gave a speech about putting men on the moon.

When they got home Nene and Granpa were already there, and they were upset. Renee felt sad that the President had died. He must have been a nice guy. Everyone seemed to really like him.

A few days later there was a funeral on the TV for the President and Nene saw a little boy saluting at the gravesite. When Nene asked who the little boy was and who the lady and the little girl at the gravesite were Nene said the little boy was the President's son, the little girl was the President's daughter, and the woman was the President's wife. Renee felt so sad she wanted to cry. This little boy and girl no longer had a Daddy, and their Mommy was sad. Everybody at the funeral seemed sad. It was a sad time; Renee would never forget that sad day.

Life finally went back to normal, and Renee went back to school. Things did not really change although it did seem more students talked to her because of what happened to the President.

Even though students talked to her occasionally, she still ended up with the black and brown crayon and bad school reports.

Renee had to repeat the first grade and Nene told her she had better hand in all the correct answers to her math and spelling problems and she better not color everything with black and brown.

Renee did not like it when Nene was mad, so she made sure she turned in correct answers and she rushed to the front of the class to get one or two acceptable crayon colors. She learned black and brown crayons were not acceptable.

Renee had to repeat the first grade. She had a whole new class and teacher, and this teacher seemed nicer. Renee felt she would do better with this teacher, she seemed to take her under her wing. She was doing better in the first grade when she repeated it. She liked her new first grade class more, but the children still shied away from her or maybe she shied away from them. Maybe it was because this was Renee's second time in the first grade. She was seven years old—a year older than most students. She only knew she had no friends in school. She at least did well with the math and reading and music.

Renee was seven now, and Aunt China would take her to fun places. Her favorite was the movie theater in town. It was only a short walk, and she and Aunt China would walk to see their favorite movies. Renee's favorite movie this year was *Chitty Chitty Bang Bang*. It was about a magical car that used to win races until it caught fire. The car went through a lot, but with the help of many people, it was going to be restored to its days of glory. It was going to be magical again.

There were adults and kids in the movie. Renee looked around. It looked like most of the people were families. There were Moms, Dads, and kids. She liked movies such as *Planet of the Apes* and *The Odd Couple*.

She was always excited to go to the cinema with Aunt China, but she wished she could go to movies with families like the other kids.

It was hard to remember Aunt China was only sixteen. She was a cross between a sister and mother. Nene and Granpa started taking her and Aunt China to the drive-in movies, they took them to see a James Bond movie called *Goldfinger* but that terrified Renee.

All she could remember was a lady being killed and painted gold! It was the scariest thing she had ever seen, she didn't even like the movie theme song Goldfinger. She liked the gadgets James Bond used in the movies, but she didn't like the killing. Shirley Bassey singing Goldfinger haunted her dreams, she had nightmares of people dying and being painted gold.

CHAPTER 5
Renee's Other Grandparents

Renee has brothers?

Aunt China didn't only take her to movies, she also walked her over to her other Grandmothers house which was not a far walk. Aunt China told her how this grandmother was her mother's mother. This grandmother lived at a different house and her name was also named Nene, but this other grandfather's name was Papa.

This grandmother and grandfather had different last names; they were not Bobson's; their last name was Boye like Renee's mother's last name. This grandmother's name was Mellie, and the grandfather's name was Claude. Mellie was a housewife who doted on her family.

As a child, Mellie played with a handmade doll who she dearly loved, she was the mother, and her doll was the daughter who went everywhere with her. Her one true dream was to be a mother with a big family.

Mellie's mother, Martha, had the same dream, she wanted to have a husband and children who all lived together in the same house.

It was said Martha, Mellie's Mom was born in the 1860s right before emancipation, she heard stories about slavery through her mother and she did not want it for her children.

Mellie's dream came true, she had the husband, a house for her large family and the freedom to go where she chose but she did not feel free. She found she was still in a sort of prison. She had to depend on her husband for everything, even decisions concerning the children; she had to care for the children, but she could not make decisions without the approval of her husband Claude. She could not go anywhere with her children without approval, she did not think it would be like this, she could not even finish High school; she was expected to stay at home to watch the children.

In the past when the children were young, Mellie had to get psychiatric help, she was admitted to a psychiatric hospital early in her marriage. Her children basically had to be raised by her husband who was a busy preacher and her oldest Daughter Penelope or Penny.

Penny had just finished high school and she was engaged to be married but she stepped up to take care of her brothers and sisters when her mother was "away" for two years.

It was a difficult time for the Boye family, the children grew up very quickly; they didn't seem to have much supervision, their father had his own church, and he was always busy with church business. Their father may been away most of the time, but he was strict when he was home, the Boye children did not stray, they did as they were told. They did not depart from the path laid out for them.

Mellie was released from the hospital and it looked like everything was back to normal, once again they were one big happy family.

She became a housewife and exceptional mother once again, she made sure she never showed anything but a happy, stable homemaker. After a few years some of the children had married, and she had lots of grandchildren who would visit weekly, her children and grandchildren were obedient, successful and respectful. One Son was a Doctor, one was a teacher, and one was a scientist.

The girls were all housewives as expected and a few were even secretaries in large corporations. The girls usually worked part time and were home in time to watch their children.

The grandchildren were the model of good behavior and civility. The Boye home was a home of peace, love, tranquility and celebration. Everyone smiled and celebrated. Nene Mellie was wonderfully calm and pleasant; it was a welcome change from Nene Bobson's house. There was one thing Renee found strange about Nene Mellie, Renee wondered why Nene Mellie muttered under her breath whenever Papa Boye was in the same room, and Renee could not understand it. Papa was so hardworking, and he was always nice and kind. He never came into her room at night and he never spoke an unkind word to anyone. She could never understand Nene's mutterings about Papa. She would mutter things like "there he is, the devil" or "the king of deceit has walked into the room."

Renee never understood and when she asked Nene Boye what she meant she would never explain, she would always say it's ok don't worry. Renee learned years later her Brother heard the same sentiments. She would not know Nene Boye's true story for decades.

She could only guess from the perspective of a young child. She only knew Nene Boye always had Papa's breakfast ready for him every morning and she waited on him hand and foot like a dutiful wife should. Whenever Renee stayed overnight there was always half of a grapefruit, a bowl of grapenuts and a slice of toast at Papas place at the kitchen table. There was also a little white pill for diabetes, Renee wondered if that's why most of the people in her family had diabetes. Her mother had diabetes and so did her aunts and uncles on her mother's side of the family.

Papa Claude was a preacher much like his Father Harvey, his father was born and freed during emancipation; there had always been a church for black people in his family.

His grandfather had started a church in Delaware in the early 1800s, the church had started to integrate a few years later, the poorer white community, along with the black community would go to the little church in Delaware. The church branched out and they added more churches which had been in the family for over a century, it was a way of life for the Boye family. Papa Boye not only maintained the church in Dorsey PA, but he was also on the church board of other churches in the district.

He had come a long way from the days he used to drive a produce truck. Before he took over the church, he uses to buy produce and poultry from farms, and he drove a meat and vegetable truck.

He would drive the truck into all the neighborhoods and sell goods at discount prices to his neighbors. Neighbors would always get meat and produce from the truck; the price was always fair. Sometimes Papa Boye would have potato chips on the truck and children would run out to the truck when it was in their neighborhood. The potato chips were always homemade in wax paper, Nene Boye had made them. They were a delicious treat, all the kids looked forward to them.

The Boye and Bobson women both had a lucrative side business with food.

Papa Boye also worked at the shipyard like Granpa Bobson, but he did not work there long, Papa had dreams of running his own church, Granpa Bobson had dreams of being a master builder; they both accomplished their dream.

It seems both men ended up in the jobs they always wanted, Renee wondered if the men ever wanted more. They certainly wanted more of their children, they both made sure their children went to school, especially the boys. The problem is expectations are not always met, sometimes their children took a different path.

Nene Boye's family seemed very loving, they never yelled, and Nene Boye always made delicious cakes.

There was always a birthday celebration and a birthday cake for one of the aunts or uncles or one of the grandchildren. There were a lot of aunts and uncles; eight to be exact. She couldn't even count the number of grandchildren; there were so many.

Whenever Renee was at their house Papa Boye would come home in the evenings and sit quietly and watch the celebrations, the entire family would be there for the birthday celebrations of one of the cousins or Aunts or Uncles.

This house was nice also, the living room had a nice brown velvet sofa, easy chairs and tables. There were no plastic covers at this house. They were friendly with the neighborhood and well liked.

The dining room was the nicest place in the house, the table was shiny wood with lace tablecloths and there were three break fronts with dishes, dolls and Knick knacks. It was a nice, warm, cozy place and everyone could sit there and talk and eat. Renee noticed her mother was never there. She wondered why.

She also found out she had two brothers who lived with her mother. She didn't know where they lived but she sure would like to meet them. She wondered why she never saw her mother or brothers.

Renee loved to comb Nene Boye's hair; it seemed this grandmother loved having her hair combed. Renee would talk to Nene Boye about her mother while combing her hair.

They would talk about her mother being shy and stuttering during school and having hair down her back. It seemed like they always talked about her mother's looks and shyness. They never talked about her mother in relation to her children. When she asked why her mother didn't live at home anymore, she was told she has her own apartment. There was never a lot of information about her mother.

Renee slept over this grandmother's house sometimes, the difference was she was never allowed to sleep in the grandmother or grandfather's bed in this house. Nene Boye explained it was inappropriate for little children to sleep in beds with adults. Renee never told Nene Boye how she slept with Nene Bobson and Granpa Bobson in the past, she was too embarrassed.

Nene Boyes and Papa Boyes room had separate twin beds, and one dresser; it was a nice room and Renee could visit, but she couldn't stay there. She always slept in a different room in a bed by herself at Nene Boye's house and one of her cousins would be in a separate bed in the room. Renee and her cousin would play with toys and watch TV, and run around the house, it was always a nice visit.

This family was different than Grandma Bea's family. In this family Uncle Junior was a Doctor, Uncle Reggie was a Teacher and Uncle Ernie was a teacher.

All the Aunts in this family were housewives with part time jobs, they didn't work full time outside the home like her other grandmother Bea. It seemed like Grandmother Bea had newer furniture and the street they lived on was wider and bigger but Nene Boye's house seemed more welcoming. Renee wondered why Nene Bobson's house was more expensive in a nicer neighborhood, she guessed it was because Papa Boye was a preacher, maybe they didn't make as much money and the Aunts and Uncles didn't live at home.

She was usually only allowed to stay at this grandmother's house for one night and Uncle Reggie would walk her home.

She was always sad to leave this grandmother's house. It was the one place where she didn't feel timid or different, and it was also a place where she never got visits at night.

One day Renee was in the kitchen with Nene Bobson eating one of her fantastic chicken dinners, she asked Nene why she never met her Brothers. Nene said they live in a different apartment, but she would meet them.

Nene and Aunt China started talking about her Brothers. They told her how her brothers lived with her Mom in a different house, they were three and four and Nene and Aunt China explained how they were going to come live with them.

She wondered why they weren't going to stay with Mommy, she wondered why she couldn't stay with Mommy, but she was excited; she would finally have little kids in this house to play with. Maybe Mommy and Daddy would eventually live with them.

It seemed like years went by, but it was only one year. Renee was seven and in the second grade. She was going to be eight soon and she was doing better in school, but she still had a problem making friends.

She did have one friend; she was a little blonde girl with blue eyes whose name was Cindy. Cindy was her first friend; she didn't treat her differently, Renee even told her about her two brothers. Cindy even invited her to her house for lunch and Nene said it was okay.

Cindy's Mom had blonde hair and blue eyes just like Cindy, she made the most delicious food. She said it was tomato soup and grilled cheese, Renee loved it; she didn't get this kind of food at home. Food at home was good, it was fried chicken and fish and roast beef and none of the food was from a can. Soups at Nene Bobson's house were always homemade. Renee liked the soup in the can she wished she could get it at home!

When Renee went home, she saw two little boys in the house playing with toy cars on the carpet, she asked who they were and she was told they were her brothers and they were now living with her, Nene, Granpa and Aunt China.

Her brothers were four and five. Their names were Reggie and Roy just like her father and grandfather. Roy was four and Reggie was five. They were funny and active. Roy was a dark cream color like Nene and Aunt China and Granpa. Reggie was Walnut colored like Renee. They were thin with big eyes and wide smiles and Renee loved them, she was a big sister and they followed her and listened to her. They were signed up for Kindergarten and the first grade and they walked to school with Renee and the neighbors. Reggie and Roy seemed to do better in school, and they made friends easily.

They came home with pages from coloring books, they were rather good at coloring, they used bright, bold colors and they stayed in the lines. They obviously did not have a problem getting to the front of the room to get the bright colored crayons.

Life seemed better in the house with Aunt China, Reggie Jr and Little Roy. Nene was strict, you had to clean up after yourself, you had to do well in school, and you had to obey. If you did what Nene said things ran smoothly. If you really wanted to get on Nene's good side, you had to compliment her cooking. She loved cooking for everyone, and she loved praise for the food she cooked. She glowed when people praised her cooking.

Praise for her cooking were not just empty praises, Nene could really cook; people came from all over Pennsylvania for Nene's cooking. She had lots of friends and she always said she would sell dinners at a restaurant one day.

CHAPTER 6
Why Does Granpa Only Tuck Renee in at Night?

The days of singing and family gatherings are more fun than the nights.

Renee didn't like going in the bed with Nene and Granpa anymore. She was eight now, but Granpa would come tuck her in when she was already in bed, but only if the people in the house were sleep or out. Renee did not like being tucked in. Granpa would always accidently touch her underpants, and it made her feel confused and angry all at once. She wondered why Granpa did not tuck anyone else in the house in. She was the only one tucked in by Granpa. She wished it would stop. Thank goodness it wasn't every night.

Renee loved having her brothers around. They would all play in the basement, which was like a playroom. They would sing songs and make believe they were in a singing group like Daddy and Aunt China. There were always a lot of singers in their house. Renee would later find out some of the singers were quite famous; as a matter of fact her daddy sang with a few famous groups.

Everyone in the family sang except Nene and Uncle Cheeks, neither had the gift of singing. Nene had the gift of cooking and business knowledge she had a head for numbers and a keen business sense. She could always cook, and she always handled the business, expenses and bills.

Uncle cheeks was in the military, he was the cool, fearless one in the family.

When Nene's brothers and sisters visited everyone would sing. The children and cousins would sing in the basement playroom and the adult aunts, uncles and great aunts and uncles would sing, play guitars and bongo drums upstairs in the house. Aunt China said singing and playing instruments went back to their great grandfather John Henry Bykerson which was Nene's maiden name.

Even their great, great grandfather Reverend Salk was musical and a fiddle player, he was born in the late 1800s! Salk was great grandmother's maiden name. All their ancestors use to sing and dance after a hard day's work and they continued to sing even now. Nene wondered if her great grandmother and her great grandfather sang in a house like this with all their family. She heard Nene talk about small log cabins with handmade wooden furniture, some people worked in the fields and some worked in the big house, she wasn't sure what the big house was or what a log cabin was.

Aunt China would take Renee, Reggie Jr and Little Roy to the park in the school yard to play on the swings and merry go round. Days in the park were always days of pure enjoyment. Renee and her brothers would take turns pushing each other on the swings and merry go rounds and they would run around the park playing tag and hide and seek. Renee was 8 and her little brothers were five and six. She did wonder why they weren't allowed to drink from the water fountain with the clean water. There was a sign near it which said, "whites only." Renee wondered what that meant.

Aunt China told them they really shouldn't drink from that water fountain; it wasn't meant for people their color; people their color had to drink from the "colored" water fountain. They didn't think this was fair, but rules were rules. The problem was the only other water in the park was a rusty pipe with rusty water and Renee and her Brothers did not want to drink rusty water. Aunt China didn't want any of them to drink from that fountain either so sometimes they would have to cut the visit to the playground short. They knew they would have to go home if they got thirsty at the park therefore, they would drink water and go to the bathroom before they left for any outing.

Reggie Jr and Little Roy did not come with a lot of belongings when they moved in, they only had a couple of outfits and a little car or truck.

They told Renee they had bikes but when they were riding them outside Mommy's house, Little Roy got hit by a car on his bike and he had to go across the street from where they lived to go to the hospital.

They said Daddy no longer lived there after that, it was only Mommy and Aunt Candy. It seems Mommy and Daddy were no longer living together when Reggie Jr. and Little Roy came to live with them. It looked like that was one of the reasons they came to live with Nene.

Little Roy's bike was broken from the accident and Reggie Jr's bike went into the garage. They did not have bikes at Nene's house, maybe they would get them when they were older. Nene and Aunt China really thought they were too young for bikes, but Daddy bought them bikes with training wheels and Aunt China, or Nene always watched them when they were riding.

The boys could not wait until they could ride bikes without training wheels, but Nene and Aunt China insisted, they weren't ready. They still had fun with the bikes, but they wanted to ride big bikes like the big boys.

Everyone was filled with anticipation and excitement; it was near Christmas. Nene and Aunt China went into the basement to get Christmas decorations and Granpa put lights up outside on the house, it was magical. He then put up the Christmas tree they bought from Don's tree lot, he would put water in the fixture in the base of the tree and then he would put lights on the tree. Once he checked the lights on the tree Nene, Aunt China and Renee would decorate the tree. This year Reggie Jr and Little Roy got to help.

After the lights, they would put shiny bulbs and ornaments on the Christmas tree, some of the ornaments were hand made by Aunt China, some were made by Renee and her brothers and some were store bought.

They would then put-on garland and tinsel and finally they would put on the star at the top of the tree. As a final touch they would put on a pink and blue shiny material called angels hair, it was itchy but beautiful. The tree was always magnificent, it looked like it towered almost to the roof. It was beautiful colors, and it twinkled all night until they went to bed. The only time it twinkled in the morning was Christmas day.

Renee always got toys for Christmas; she got clothes too, but they were no fun, she loved the toys. She couldn't wait for Christmas; she knew her brothers would get toys too. Nene and Aunt China told them how Santa would bring them presents! Her brothers were excited by Santa, but Renee didn't really believe in a jolly man who brought presents to all the boys and girls around the world.

Renee was quite sure Nene and Granpa was Santa but there was a little part of her that still believed there was a Santa, especially when she turned on the news and saw newscasters talking about him on TV! She did wonder how he could go to her house and then go to the houses of little kids in China and Africa in one night.

The night before Christmas she fell asleep and in the morning she and her brothers woke up and went downstairs to see all the presents under the Christmas tree. It was early in the morning, but Daddy was there!

The presents were from Santa (?) and they stretched out from the Christmas tree to the middle of the living room!

Aunt China would look at the tags on the gifts and hand them out to whoever's name was on the tag. Renee and her brothers got a lot of the gifts, there were a lot of clothes but there were a lot of cool gifts too. She got paper dolls, an easy bake oven and a shopping cart with food and a cash register. She loved all those gifts, but her favorites were the books.

She was eight, and she loved to read. She liked Doctor Seuss, Dick, and Jane, the comics in the papers, and comic books. Maybe there was a Santa Claus after all! Renee was thrilled with her Christmas presents, she felt there must have been a little magic involved; she got exactly what she wanted and some things she didn't even say out loud.

Her brothers got a lot of clothes too, they didn't really care about the clothes, but they loved the sets of big trucks and cars and they got rock em sock em robots! They squealed with delight and played with them for hours. The robots were in a ring and the jabbed at each other until one was knocked down, it was like a real boxing match. They got books too, but they didn't really like them, they really were not interested in reading.

Nene got boring stuff like a scarf that looked like a fox, and a big scarf that looked like a fur; they called it a fox stole and a mink stole. Nene seemed to love her gifts, but they looked boring to Renee and it was only two gifts.

Granpa got tools, clothes and cigars, they said they were expensive cigars, but Renee didn't think those were nice gifts either. Then again Renee assumed he liked them because he lit up a cigar right away and he seemed delighted, calm and relaxed.

Aunt China got records and albums, a tape player and a record player, she started dancing as soon as she opened them. The entire family was dancing to Christmas songs and popular songs. Renee thought those seemed like nice gifts, she also got clothes but unlike Renee she loved the new clothes. Not only did Aunt China dance to her new records, but she also recorded her voice on the tape player. Her and Daddy and Granpa sang on the tape recorder and they sounded rather good.

Daddy got wallet and clothes, he also got shoes and a coat; Renee was surprised at how happy he was about those gifts? Daddy loved those gifts.

Everybody seemed happy with their gifts and they had a big breakfast and lunch. Daddy had left, he said he was going back to his house to get some rest and practice songs for his singing group. They had a show on New Year's Eve.

Daddy lived in his own apartment now and Mommy lived somewhere else, Renee and her Brothers did not know where she lived. Nene and Aunt China and Granpa seemed to know where she lived but it was a big mystery for Renee and her brothers.

The rest of the family had eaten and opened gifts. They were snacking on Christmas candy and nuts when the doorbell rang.

It was Renee's mother. Renee and her brothers were shocked yet happy. She rarely came to the house; this was a special surprise. They couldn't believe their Mommy was here. Mommy came with her Brother Uncle Reggie and they had big presents! Thank goodness Nene and Aunt China reminded Renee and her brothers to get their Mommy a Christmas gift in case she stopped by on Christmas. She was glad they had gifts for Mommy!

They had gotten the gifts for everyone including Mommy from the five- and ten-cent store. Renee and her brothers saved their money in a jelly jar all year and Aunt China took them to the store to buy gifts. All together they had $15! They bought Mommy and both Nene's perfume and they bought Aunt China an album. They bought Granpa and Papa ties, they were so proud of themselves. They wrapped their gifts in wrapping paper and put them under the Christmas tree.

They couldn't wait to give Mommy her gifts. Granpa and Daddy had left and only Nene, Aunt China, Renee and her brothers were home when Mommy got to their house.

Mommy said hello to Nene and Aunt China, and she gave them a big hug. She then gave Renee and her brothers big hugs.

She told them she had presents for everyone and Renee and her brothers couldn't wait, they had their Mommy and presents! Mommy got Renee a doll which was almost as tall as she was, she could walk and talk! She was white but that was ok because Renee knew all dolls were white. Her Brothers got a great new truck which had the word Hess on it like the gas station. Mommy gave Nene perfume, and she gave Aunt China a transistor radio, they all got great gifts.

Mommy had to leave soon after that and Renee and her Brothers were a little sad, but it certainly was a great Christmas. Renee wished Mommy could be here all the time, she wished Mommy could be here when Daddy was here, but they were never here together.

She knew other kids had Mommies and Daddies who lived together because she heard about them in school, but she knew she would never get to live with her Mommy and Daddy. Those other kids in school were lucky to have a Mommy and Daddy who lived with them.

Christmases came and went, and Renee and her brothers continued to go to the elementary school, they walked with the next-door neighbors, the Houston's who had eight kids. Five of the neighbor's kids were in elementary school and Junior High; three of the kids were in high school. Renee and her brothers loved walking with the youngest boy Curtis, he was a year younger than Renee. Curtis was rambunctious, funny, smart and active, he loved to run and play; his big brother Tony and his big sister Reebie had to sometimes yell at him to get him to stop running in the street and on the sidewalks. The walk to school was never boring.

The Houston kids always walked the younger kids on the block to school, this is how Renee met her new best friend, Maggie Alice Trainor. They called Maggie Alice "Fawn" because she had huge brown eyes like a deer. She was only eight, two years younger than Renee, but they loved the same things. They loved the Fifth Dimension, Aretha Franklin, Bobby Gentry, and a lot of other artist.

They would walk to school singing "Up, Up, and Away," "Ode to Billy Joe," "Respect," and the Houston kids would join in. They would sing and play all the way to school. The Houston's and the kids on her block never teased her. She wondered if it was because all the kids on her block were the same color as her or maybe it was because they all knew her better.

Renee would laugh and sing and play with the kids on her block, she was not shy around them. Sometimes Fawn would come over her house and sit on her steps, they would look at magazines and listen to the transistor radio. They would laugh and sing and daydream about marrying one of the Jackson 5, they would take walks around the neighborhood and to the park. They were great friends, they always had fun together, but Fawn never came into Renee's house. Fawn's mother was an elementary school teacher, and she did not want fawn to go into anyone's house,

Renee was ten now and her Brothers were seven and eight. They finally all had friends outside of school. Renee had a one friend in her classroom who was blond haired and blue eyed, and she had Fawn who lived on her block. She even had another friend who walked with the Houston's and lived a block away. Her name was Dina Lutz.

Dina was one year older than Renee, and the boys were already crazy about her. Dina had skin the color of milk chocolate, she had black wavy hair down to her shoulders and she already had breast! Renee did not have breast yet. Dina swayed when she walked, and she always flashed a big bright smile. She never laughed at Renee and people didn't tease Renee when Dina was around. Dina talked about boys and music; Renee didn't know much about boys except her little brothers, but she loved talking about music. Renee loved the walk to school and the walk home, they were her favorite times of the day.

CHAPTER 7
MLK and Bobby Kennedy Were Killed!

One day Renee and Fawn were sitting on her steps singing, looking at magazines and daydreaming and it was almost time for fawn to go home. They had eaten dinner and they had done their homework, but it was Thursday, and it was a school night and they had to be in the house before 7:00 p.m. It was 6:30 p.m. and Renee heard Nene and Aunt China scream from inside the house, Fawn's mother called from down the street for her to come in the house; Renee wondered what on earth had happened.

When she got into the house the TV was on and she saw that Martin Luther king had been shot, Nene and Aunt China were beside themselves. Granpa came home and he said people were in the streets "rioting." Martin Luther King seemed like such a nice man, he always talked about everyone being equal and Renee liked that. She couldn't understand why anyone would kill him, it made her sad, afraid and angry all at once.

When she asked Aunt China why they killed him Aunt China said "because some people are prejudiced and filled with hate.

Renee wondered how a person could be so full of hate they could kill someone. She knew she could get mad sometime, but she never wanted to kill anyone. Why was there so much hate in the world? Would the hatred ever stop?

Tomorrow was Friday and Renee was a little nervous about going to school. Granpa said there was rioting in the streets. Would people riot as they walked to school? Would she, her brothers and her neighbors and friends be in danger when they walked to school tomorrow? Hopefully, they would be able to walk to school without trouble, it probably would be a quiet walk.

Everybody came over to Nene's house that night. All the neighbors, friends, and family were piled into Nene's house. They were all yelling and crying but then Bobby Kennedy came on the TV.

He made a speech about understanding how upset everyone was, he said he knew how it felt because his brother had been killed. It calmed everyone down, but they were still sad and angry.

Everyone went home but Renee figured they would still be sad and angry tomorrow and maybe even the next day.

The next day on the walk to school thank goodness the kids did not see any rioting. All the neighborhood kids talked about MLK being killed, they all knew it was a horrible, terrible, tragedy and they wondered if they would ever catch the person who killed him. Their families told them how MLK fought for colored people and they wondered if anyone would continue to fight.

They were all on the lookout for riots, but the streets were quiet at 8:00 a.m. When they got to school the killing of MLK was all any of the students talked about, but the teachers said it was a sad thing and they had to get on with the days lesson. Renee couldn't concentrate on what the teacher was saying, she could only think about MLK dying and people being upset and rioting. She couldn't remember ever being that sad and angry.

The walk home was sad and quiet, there was no playing or singing, only sadness and walking. There was no playing or singing on the block that weekend, there was only talking and anger and hopelessness. Renee and her friends didn't sing and dance and watch funny TV shows and Aunt China and her friends didn't joke and kid each other and dance around like they usually did. It was a time of sad, harsh feelings and Renee hoped these feelings would end soon.

There still was tension in the air from the killing of MLK, Renee did not think it would end but Nene and Aunt China said life still had to go on and they were talking about Easter.

Easter was two weeks away, and the somber mood was changed to hopefulness.

She and her brothers would be going shopping with Aunt China and Nene for Easter Clothes, they always liked going shopping and they loved new clothes.

Nene always made sure daddy paid money every week from his job check for extras for the kids, she and Aunt China wanted the kids to have nice clothes for school.

It was the first time they went to a department store; it was called J.C Penney's, Daddy drove them into the city to the store. The store was huge with moving steps they called escalators. There were sections for ladies' clothes, men's clothes and children clothes and they headed for the children's clothes.

Renee went with Aunt China and Nene to find a dress and the boys went with Daddy. Renee looked at the frilly dresses made of satin with lace and taffeta and she didn't like any of them. Aunt China and Nene told her she would look nice in the dresses with shiny black patent leather shoes and white gloves, but Renee did not want any of those dresses. She did not like the frilly look; she liked a more tailored modern look.

Suddenly she looked at the next rack which had dresses with matching spring coats, and she knew she found her Easter Outfit. She found a black and white checkered dress with a matching cape! She would look so glamorous and grown up in this outfit, she was after all ten years old! She asked Nene and Aunt China if she could try the dress and cape on and they said yes, Aunt China said she would look nice in it.

She tried the dress on, it had large white and black checkered blocks on it, and it came with a matching cape which came to her waist. She looked glamorous! She came out of the dressing room to show Nene and Aunt China and they loved it. Aunt China said they had to go get her a white purse and white stockings and Nene told them they couldn't forget the white gloves. They purchased the outfit, and they went to find Daddy and the boys.

The boys had gotten brown suits with white shirts and brown shoes, they were all going to be sharp for Easter, and Renee couldn't wait! To top things off, they got Easter baskets to go with their new outfits.

She was now ten and much too old to believe in the Easter bunny and Nene and Aunt China said she was right, they explained how Easter was really about Jesus. They explained how it was a celebration of him really being alive and allowing us to be closer to God.

They reminded her of how we had to try to follow him and try to behave as he would behave. They always explained how Jesus really didn't love one person's color more than the next person's color, he loved everyone and how he wanted everyone to care for one another and do what is right. She loved the idea of Jesus, she even started reading the Bible. She asked God for help whenever she read it and miracle of miracles, she understood it.

Renee knew the idea of being everyone's friend and not caring about the color of a person's skin was the right way to think and act, she never questioned it. She loved reading the Bible, and she was excited about going to church to learn more about Jesus. She loved the stories about Jesus, his miracles, wisdom and compassion. The whole family was going to church for Easter.

Renee and her brothers woke up and put on their new Easter outfits, they had taken baths the night before, they were all ready to go to church but first they took pictures with Daddy and Aunt China.

Everybody liked church except Granpa, he was always too busy for church; he was usually at the lodge or somewhere else important. Even though Granpa wasn't at church the rest of the family liked being in church. They all listened attentively to the Easter service; Renee even took notes. The preacher talked about Jesus and his disciples, it was a message of hope and new beginnings. The Easter Sermon never seemed to be long, it was full of good news although kids were excited about Easter baskets waiting at home for them after church.

People in church were still upset over the killing of Martin Luther King but Renee hoped the person who killed MLK would go to jail, and people would calm down. They had just heard a sermon about forgiveness and turning the other cheek. Maybe people would get along better after the Easter Holiday.

Renee worried there would never be another leader like Martin Luther King but as a matter of fact, it looked like another Civil Rights leader named Jesse Jackson had worked with MLK. He always fought for equal rights and people thought he might continue the fight for equality and justice. Things were starting to look better.

Thursday, June 5, Renee, Fawn, and Dina Lutz were walking home from school. They were excited about a county fair at the high school on the weekend. There would be rides, cotton candy and games. Dina said there would be music and boys there and they could all talk to them at the fair.

Fawn didn't think the boys would like her, but Dina assured her one boy did like her. His name was Donny Timber. He was the only other colored boy in her classroom and he always teased her. She didn't think he liked her, but Dina did seem to know a lot.

Renee was kind of excited to go to the fair the next day. June 5, 1968, was going to be a fun day! Renee, Fawn, and Dina all went home to their houses excited about the next day.

Renee did her homework, her and her Brothers and Nene and Granpa watched the Beverly Hillbillies and the Carol Burnett show. It was a good day and a great evening, Renee went to bed and she had pleasant dreams about carnival rides, snacks, music and boys.

Renee woke up the next morning excited about the carnival and Aunt China was already downstairs. Aunt China was nineteen now and no longer in school. She graduated last year. She worked in a factory which made designer clothes. Dina was surprised Aunt China wasn't working in a big building making a lot of money. She was smart, pretty, and people always followed her. She was a great leader.

She was sure she could get a better paying job in a nice office; she had gotten excellent grades and she excelled in typing in school. Aunt China was looking for a secretarial position, in one of the major companies but they were impossible to get. She thought she would be working for a business executive, but she didn't complain. She loved her job in the factory. She could get designer clothes for cheap, and she always brought some home for Renee and Nene.

Aunt China always went to work before Renee went to school. Renee was surprised to see her still at home when she went down for breakfast.

Reggie Jr and Little Roy were still getting dressed when Renee went downstairs, she was hungry; she loved Trix, and Coco Puffs cereal and she was hoping Nene would let her have cereal this morning.

When she walked into the kitchen Renee immediately knew something was drastically wrong. Nene and Aunt China looked devastated. Renee asked what was wrong and why was Aunt China still at home, she usually left for work before now. She noticed Nene and Aunt China were listening to the radio, when Renee listened, she heard the announcer say, "For those of you just tuning in, Robert Kennedy has been shot."

Renee couldn't believe it, not the nice man whose Brother JFK had died. Not the nice man who told everybody he understood about people being upset when MLK died. This couldn't be that Robert Kennedy. Renee felt physically ill, tremendously sad and more than a little angry. She couldn't believe it, she still wondered why people were so filled with hate, and she wondered why people wanted to hurt other people. She was so confused, and nobody seemed to have answers. Granpa had gone to work but Aunt China was taking the day off. Nene still made Renee eat, she allowed her to eat Trix because she needed her strength to go to school. Reggie Jr and Little Roy came downstairs to eat, they were excited about eating cereal and going to school.

They weren't as upset over Robert Kennedy's shooting; they were sad but not devastated. They were only eight and nine years old. Maybe they didn't understand. Renee thought maybe he wouldn't die, and everything would be okay. Maybe they thought the same thing.

When Renee got to school the talk in the school yard was about Robert Kennedy, all the children and teachers were crying. When they finally went inside the schoolhouse the teachers were too upset to continue with the lesson. They listened to the radio and the lesson was about the Kennedys. Renee was glad they got to talk about the Kennedys, but she wondered why they didn't do that with MLK.

They did go home early like they did with MLK and Renee, Fawn and Dina talked about the Kennedy's. They talked about how nice Bobby Kennedy was when MLK died, they couldn't believe he had been shot.

They agreed they no longer wanted to go to the fair, they even wondered if there would be a fair, it looked like there would be another sad weekend. The next day was Friday, what if Bobby Kennedy died on a Friday? Didn't JFK die on a Friday too? Could the two Brothers in the same family die on the same day even if it was different years?

That evening everyone watched the news of Bobby Kennedy shooting and they prayed he would not die. They watched it on the color TV, Renee almost wished they could watch it on black and white TV. The color TV made everything more vivid and real, they kept showing his wife saying, "Save Bobby."

The next morning was no better. The Bobson family learned Bobby Kennedy had died the night before at 12:15 a.m. which was Friday morning, He died Friday morning just like his Brother JFK.

Renee wondered how the Kennedy family felt. She knew Bobby Kennedy had children. Would one of his Sons salute at his funeral like at JFKs funeral? Two days after Bobby Kennedy died, Aunt China told Renee his funeral train would be coming through their town. The train started at New York and it would end in Washington, DC.

They walked to the train tracks and a huge crowd had gathered, some were waving flags, and some had signs and pictures of Bobby Kennedy. As the train came into the Dorsey PA station it did not stop but it slowed down. The huge crowd was silent, and faces were sad and tired. It seemed the whole town was in mourning. After the train passed and it could no longer be seen everyone went back to their homes to watch the train pass on the news. Renee thought it was eerily quiet, sad and strange. Aunt China told Renee a train usually takes four hours to go from New York to Washington DC, but it took eight hours that day. Renee wondered how it could take twice as long without stopping.

This seemed like a violent world to Renee. She hoped no other great men were killed. She hoped there would be no more riots and she hoped no one else would be hurt or killed in a riot. She couldn't wrap her head around it, but it seemed like the men killed were colored or they agreed with colored people's rights of being equal. It looked to her like some people did not want people to be equal. It made her sad, confused and determined. Renee agreed with all those people who thought all people of all colors should be equal.

Renee thought 1968 had to be the worst year in history but Aunt China told her about the previous year 1967. It was Aunt China's senior year in high school, and she would soon graduate. Aunt China was going to Senior dances, senior proms and the senior graduation ceremony which would be a major highlight in her life, but she was also aware of the riots across America that year.

There were riots in most cities in America but there was a horrible riot in Newark NJ which started over police officers beating a black man. That riot continued when a police officer shot and killed a woman through her window in her apartment. It ended up with over twenty people dead and hundreds seriously injured.

The black citizens in the city were already upset before the riots because businesses would not hire them for work and apartment complexes would not house them. There was also a riot in Washington DC in 1967 about the Vietnam War. People rioted, and some even got into a place called the Pentagon; they threw rocks, vegetables and anything they could get their hands on. It was a miracle no one was killed in that riot.

Even Muhammad Ali protested the Vietnam War and refused to be drafted, he said he couldn't go fight people who were as dark as him when blacks were treated badly in America. There were also riots in a place called Detroit where people were hurt and killed. 1967 was a violent year. Aunt China would always remember it because it was the year she graduated high school. There seemed to be a lot of violence in the 1960s, Renee hoped it would stop.

CHAPTER 8
Family Trip Back to Ancestral Roots

What's an outhouse?

Life went back to being somewhat normal again. It was summer break and school was out. Nene and Granpa took Renee, her brothers, and Aunt China to Maryland to visit their uncle Randy and his wife Aunt Laney. Uncle Randy was really Nene's Cousin, so he was really Renee's cousin, but they called him and his wife Aunt Laney and Uncle Randy. Granpa had gotten a new mint green Chevy and he drove them all to Maryland.

The family was thrilled about the trip, they got to look at the countryside and they even got to stop to get food. Nene made sure they only stopped at places that were listed in her little green book. When Rene asked Nene why they could only go places which were listed in the green book Nene said they were places they could all go safely, and they had the best food. When Renee asked why they wouldn't be safe, Nene explained how some white people in certain towns did not want colored people in their stores or restaurants. Aunt China said there were people like that in Dorsey also that's why they couldn't eat at the five-and-ten counters.

Renee certainly was glad they had that little green book. They never rode anywhere far without the Atlas and the little green book. It was strange, when Renee asked the white kids in her class about the little green book, none of them seemed to know what she was talking about. They thought she was being weird again. They didn't know about a book which listed places where they could all go to get the best food.

It seemed like it took hours to ride to Maryland, but Renee and her Brothers loved it, they would count cows and sing old McDonald, they sawhorses and chickens; it was great.

When they finally arrived in Maryland, they saw signs which said welcome to Princess Mary. Nene explained how the town of Princess Mary was all their relatives, she said everyone in the town was related. Renee didn't understand how they could all be related but Aunt China seemed to understand. She said it went all the way back to the 1800s.

She told a story about a long time ago when some of her people were freed from slavery. It was rumored there were slaves in the family who were owned by a President in the Whitehouse and Nene agreed. The freed slaves saved their money from playing the fiddle and singing in the Whitehouse and neighboring communities. Renee wondered if that is where her father and Aunt China got their singing talent.

It seems her ancestors, the freed slaves saved enough to buy land and they ended up buying the land in a small town, that town was Princess Mary. It seems her people had been moving to that town for over a century.

Princess Mary was a small town, there was a lot of farmland with cows, pigs, mules and chickens. There was a general store on the corner and there was a movie theatre, a town hall and a church. It was green with beautiful trees and the houses were far apart. It was quite different from the town of Dorsey PA.

The houses in Dorsey were close together, they were called row houses, and they had small, manicured lawns. These were big houses with large front lawns and expansive backyards.

When they finally pulled up to Uncle Randy's house Renee couldn't believe how beautiful it was. The house seemed to be a city block long. It was a one story, but it was still one of the biggest houses she had ever seen. The front lawn was exceptionally large, it seemed to frame the entire front of the house and go on past the house. There were all kinds of flowers, tulips, rose bushes, and plants Renee couldn't name.

Nene and Granpa explained how all the men in the family helped Uncle Randy build the house, it really was a family house.

They didn't use outside contractors or electricians, men in the family who knew about plumbing organized the plumbing, and men in the family who know about electric installation installed the electricity. Granpa knew about carpentry from working in the shipyard, he organized the builders. All the men did the landscaping when the women told them what the gardens and lawn should look like. Renee could not believe Granpa, and her Uncles built this house. Nene said their family have been building houses since the 1800s, they built cabins and big houses for the plantation owners.

Nene, Granpa, Renee and her Brothers got out of the car. Renee, her brothers and Aunt Chine went to explore in the back yard while Nene and Granpa went in the house with Uncle Randy and Aunt Laney.

The back yard was much bigger than the front lawn, there was a host of animals including chickens, cows and a couple of pigs. They probably could have had horses if they wanted them.

It was not only as wide as the front lawn, but it went all the way back to what seemed like the highway.

The pigs were in the back yard in a square wooden box which was called a pen, the cows were far off in the field, the chickens were in what they called a coop, but a few were running around in the back yard. Renee and her Brothers were ecstatic, they were chasing chickens and calling the pigs; they had never seen anything like it.

Finally, Aunt China, Renee and her brothers grew tired of chasing animals and they went inside the house.

The inside of the house was huge, Renee couldn't believe how big the house was on the inside. There was a large kitchen with lots of cabinets, drawers and contraptions Renee had never seen. There were butter churns, meat grinders and big pots with strange lids for making jelly. There were old fashioned contraptions, but there were new freezers, stoves and refrigerators. It was very neat and clean; it was old fashioned, yet it had all the newest appliances.

There were plenty of rooms for everyone to sleep, the house had five bedrooms, but Renee wanted to sleep in the huge living room with Aunt China, her brothers and her two cousins. It was like camping out except they were inside.

There were only a few things Renee did not like about the house. It seemed whenever she turned on the tap water it smelled like eggs, it smelled so bad she did not want to drink it.

Nene explained it was well water and there was nothing healthier than well water. She said it had natural iron and minerals, it was the healthiest water you could drink.

They also drank cow's milk straight from the cow which tasted funny to Renee. Of course, Nene said cow milk straight from the cow was the best milk; it was extremely healthy. She said it was not processed, it had no added chemicals and it was good for you, she proudly exclaimed, you couldn't get milk like that in a supermarket!

Meals included meat which was kept in the smoke house near the house. Renee later learned the meat came from animals that were once in the yard, she might have been playing with the animals! She didn't like to think of the animals ending up on the dinner table, but Nene asked her where she thought they got chicken and beef for the supermarket?

The worst thing about the house was there was no bathroom inside! There was an outhouse outside in the back yard, but Renee did not even know what an outhouse was. She was told an outhouse was a bathroom outside, it's how people went to the bathroom before indoor plumbing was invented. She did not want to go into the outhouse, the thought terrified her. What if there were snakes there? What if she needed to use the bathroom at night? She dreaded the outhouse, but she decided she might as well go to the bathroom before it got dark. Thank goodness it didn't get dark until 8:00 p.m. She went at 7:30 p.m.

The outhouse was a little red wooden building in the backyard. When you opened the door it did not smell good. The smell was horrible; she did not even know how to describe the smell. It smelled like urine, number two, and chemicals. She could imagine the smell attracting all kinds of creepy, crawly animals. *What if there was a snake in the toilet?* Luckily, there was no snake, but she certainly wasn't going to dawdle in there.

The outhouse had no sink; there was only a makeshift toilet which was a hole surrounded by a box which contained a toilet seat on top of the box. She quickly sat down and did number one. Thank goodness she didn't have to do number two; it would take longer. She finished in record time. You could not flush it but at least there was toilet paper. She finished, and she quickly went outside. You had to wash your hands with the hose outside. The hose was next to the outhouse and she used it to wash her hands, there was also lye soap which she tried to use but she didn't like the smell. She was glad she washed her hands; she didn't want to touch the doorknob of the house with dirty hands. She knew she would wait until morning to use the outhouse again.

The outhouse and water were two of Renee's least favorite things about the house in Maryland, but it was still a great place to be. Renee thought they went there for vacation, but Nene and Aunt China told her how the men went there to work on the house while the family was visiting. The women would be cooking, the children would be out playing, and the men would be working on finishing the bathroom plumbing, woodwork and hardware on the house.

The children would not only play in the yard in Maryland, but they would also tour the town. Renee, her brothers, and her cousins would walk into town with Aunt China and get candy and soda pop at the corner grocery store, they would also go to the movies and to the park. One of the movies playing was *Planet of the Apes*. They all loved that movie and recited lines when the movie was over.

It was almost 7:00 p.m. and time to walk back to the house. They did not have to return until dark. They were fine if they got to Uncle Randy's house in the evening before dusk. There were no streetlights; it got very dark after dusk; they knew they needed to be back way before then.

When they got back to the house it would be dinnertime. The food was good, but Renee wondered if they were eating chicken which use to be in the yard, she wanted to go outside to make sure the chickens were still there, she had counted them, she would know if one was missing. The chicken tasted and looked different to her, Nene said it's because its fresh chicken, she assured Renee it was taken from the freezer. Renee still thought it tasted different.

After dinner, the workday was done, and the men talked about the progress made on the house building and the plans for the next day's installations and improvements.

The women talked about cooking and preparations for the meal for the next day which included killing or decapitating chickens and slaughtering a pig. The children weren't required to watch but they could if they wanted to. Renee didn't want to watch or eat the meat.

Renee was glad when the talk about slaughtering stopped. The mood turned jovial, and the men grabbed banjos, guitars and bongos, and everyone would sing. It was a loud, boisterous time of laughter and fun, everybody would sing and dance into the night.

Renee had a few problems such as the outhouse and water when they visited Uncle Randy, country living was quite different than her little town in Pennsylvania, but Maryland was a nice place to be for family gatherings. The house in Maryland and the little town where all her family and ancestors lived made Renee feel like she was a part of something bigger than herself.

They stayed with Uncle Randy for a week, they would watch as her cousins fed the animals, they would get up early to feed the chickens, pigs, and milked the cows. Renee, her brothers and Aunt China were impressed when their cousins milked the cows. They were very quick and skillful, and it was interesting to watch. It was entertaining to watch the milking of cows, but Renee didn't think the milk tasted good.

Sometimes Nene and Uncle Robbie's wife who they called Cousin Laney would take the kids into town in the big brown station wagon.

Nene and cousin Laney took the kids into town to get groceries and plants, the kids had a great time going up and down the aisle of the grocery store and garden center. Aunt Laney drove because she was familiar with the area and the sites in the town. She pointed out different sites such as signs which had the dates of when a town was founded, and she pointed out where one town began and one ended. She loved recounting family history and how they all had ancestors which dated back to the founding of the town, there were even special papers with the family name Bykerson connected to the founding of the town.

It was fascinating, all the kids were talking about the origins of the town when they noticed geese walking across the street. Cousin Laney and Nene said, "Look at those big geese"!

Cousin Laney hit one of the geese "by accident" with the car. At first, she and Nene were dismayed but then they said, "That sure is a big goose, that's a Christmas dinner goose"! They didn't want to leave the dead goose there, so they put him in a bag in the back seat!

Renee was mortified, did they run over the goose on purpose?! Was this an everyday occurrence? Was she riding with poultry killers? Was this a fowl execution enterprise, were they really riding with a goose body? Were they going to cook the goose? Renee started to feel lightheaded, she would never get use to country life. Did all country people live like this or was it just cousin Laney and Nene? Nene seemed quite comfortable with it.

They got back to cousin Laney's house and she and Nene cut, plucked and dressed the goose! It went into the freezer, at least they didn't have it for dinner, Renee was grateful for that.

Finally, the week was over, and it was time to go back home to Dorsey Pennsylvania. Nene had a lot of food for the road, but she still made sure she had the little green book in case they needed to stop.

They all piled into the Chevy and Granpa started the drive back home. They still remarked on the cows, horses and pigs they passed on the drive home but there were not as many games. They did use the green book to find a place for dinner, they had delicious hot sausage sandwiches with fried onions and homemade potato chips. The meal brightened the mood, but it was not as jovial as the ride to Uncle Randy's. Renee wondered why it was always sad to leave a place to go back home. Maybe it was the lack of anticipation or maybe it was the thought of going back to the same thing day after day.

Even her brothers seemed to be less jovial and less animated, as a matter of fact they slept for most of the ride home after they stopped for dinner.

They finally arrived home and their dog Foxy greeted them at the door, his tail was wagging as he jumped up and down. Foxy was so excited to see them, he kept running back and forth, it's almost like he was trying to kiss everyone. Renee loved Foxy, he was always happy to see everyone, and he was never mean or vicious. Nene made sure one of the Houston boys who lived next door walked foxy and fed him while they were gone, and it looked like he did a good job. Foxy looked healthy and happy to see his family again.

No one was hungry because they had stopped at a bar/restaurant listed in Nene's green book, everyone was ready to go to bed but first they had to unpack their clothes.

Reggie Jr and Little Roy went to their room, they unpacked their bags and put the clothes in their dresser drawers and Renee and Aunt China went to their room to unpack and put their clothes away. Nene had washed the family's clothes at Uncle Randy's house in an old washing machine with a ringer, she then hung them on a clothesline outside, she was glad everyone came home with clean clothes. Nene used to have a ringer washing machine, and she used to hang the wet clothes on a clothesline outside, but she finally got a modern washing machine and a clothes dryer. She didn't miss the days of the ringer washing machine, but she still liked the clothes drying on the clothesline outside.

Once everyone in the family had put their clothes away it was time for bed, Renee was so glad to go to sleep and she was glad Aunt China wasn't going out. She liked it when Aunt China was in the next bed, there were never any visits when Aunt China was in the room; it was a nice peaceful, restful night. She dreamt of beautiful houses with big green lawns and horses and buggies and ladies in hoop gowns.

The brown people in her dream were singing, dancing and cooking, their gowns weren't as big, but their faces looked happier.

1968 was a sad year. Aunt China talked about student protest which were still going on all over the world. She said people were still protesting about the Vietnam War, which was the war in which their cousin was killed. He was only nineteen. He used to visit them every month especially in the summer. He was hilarious and quite the prankster. Renee loved when he came to visit, then he went to Vietnam and never came back. There was a hole in the entire family when he was killed, it would never be the same.

It seemed a lot of young men were killed in Vietnam; it was always on the news. The entire year seemed to be killings and demonstrations, but Aunt China and Nene were sure the war was going to end soon. Renee certainly hoped it would end, she didn't want anyone else to be killed.

The summer seemed long and hot, and Renee and her brothers loved to go outside to play. They would meet up with neighborhood children and play, tag, hopscotch, red light/green light and house. Sometimes Renee and Fawn would sit on the steps and play jacks, there was always a game to play outside or places to explore in town. It was a hot summer, but it felt wonderful to sit under the big maple tree with Fawn and a few other neighborhood girls. They would play with paper dolls and they would have tea parties and listen to music on the transistor radio. Those were carefree summer days although Nene sometimes dreaded the nights, she hated it when Aunt China wasn't in the room when it was time to sleep.

The summer was over, and it was time to go back to school, Renee was excited, Nene had bought her and her brothers new school clothes plus Aunt China bought clothes from the factory, she always went to school dressed in the latest styles.

She was tall and thin, and the clothes showed off her long legs and tiny waist, some kids complimented her, but some girls acted like they hated her.

Aunt China said they were jealous because she had the latest styles and they looked good on her.

She liked walking to school with her friends Fawn and Dina and maybe she would even have more friends this year. She hoped her teacher would be nice and interesting, she was filled with anticipation. Her brothers were also excited, they made friends with some of the neighborhood boys, and they wondered if the boys would be in their classes. They were ready to practically run out the door on the first day of school.

CHAPTER 9
School's in Session

Why are some people so mean?

School was different, Renee was in the fourth grade now and her teacher's name was Mr. Warner. It was the first time Renee had a man for a teacher, he was kind, he treated every student equally, he taught them long division and fractions and Renee was exceptionally good at it although her favorite subject was English.

She wondered why so many of the students didn't like him, when she asked them, they said he had never married, and he never had a girlfriend for as long as he taught in the elementary school and he taught for years.

Renee couldn't understand why people disliked him because he never married. He was very smart, kind and a lot of fun, he was the most intelligent, knowledgeable teacher in the school; she didn't understand why people didn't like him. She thought there were mean students in her class who didn't like a lot of people. Some students were very mean no matter who you were.

Renee was very thin no matter what she ate, and the children laughed at her for that, but she still did very well in school that year. She got all A's and good comments on her report card, it was a great year in school, except for mean girls who teased her and everyone else who wasn't a part of the special group. As a matter of fact, it seemed like there were a lot of students in the mean girl group, even boys. The entire group were what Nene and Aunt China called mean white people.

They explained it's not all white people, some people will call you nasty names, they get it from their parents; you can ignore them but if anybody tries to hit you, hit them back! They taught her not to take crap from anyone, she shouldn't hit first but she should sure defend herself.

There were also white kids in the group who were teased because they were not "well off" they didn't have the newest shoes and clothes; they didn't live in the biggest houses or the best part of town. Renee heard students call them "poor white trash." She thought that was mean and unacceptable, but they never did anything to defend themselves.

Renee was friendly to all the kids even if they were not friendly to her if they didn't threaten her, she didn't cause problems. One girl who was picked on who was not "well off" was a white girl who invited Renee to her house for lunch. They always played together at recess and talked about one of Renee's favorite subjects' food! She loved having lunch at the girl's house, Nene allowed it and Renee was glad.

Renee also noticed red flags with a blue X with stars on her walk home from her school. They didn't look like the American Flag Granpa put out on fourth of July or Memorial Day, he was proud of the American flag because he was an army veteran who served in WWII. Some of her classmates carried flags with the blue x. It must have been OK because the teacher never said anything.

Aunt China and Nene explained the flags and they talked about why some of the students tended to be mean. They pointed out how Renee and her brother and black kids on the block had to play in the back yard. Aunt China described how the white kids on the next street would pick fights if they saw black kids in the front of their own house. When black kids played in their own front yards white kids would tell them to get out of the neighborhood. Black kids from the neighborhood started to fight back. They decided to play in their back and front yards. They started playing in the front and back of their houses; they would not be bullied.

Renee never noticed, she did notice white kids and black kids did not play together in her neighborhood, but she didn't think about it.

She also ignored the mean comments in school, she didn't even realize the comments about watermelon and fried chicken were mean. She loved watermelon and friend chicken, she thought everybody did. She concentrated on being an A student and making Nene and Aunt China proud. The best thing about that year was the absence of the late-night visits. Renee could finally get a good night's sleep; it might be because someone was always home because Aunt China's friends started coming over and listening to records at the house.

Aunt China would go out on the weekends at night sometimes but Granpa would also be out on the weekend at nights. Maybe the visits stopped because Nene stayed up late, Renee didn't know why they stopped but it was such a relief.

She did notice how Nene and Granpa would argue when Granpa got home from the lodge on the weekends. Sometimes the arguments would be quite violent, they would wake Renee up.

One-time Nene had to go to the doctor the next day but so did Granpa. They would yell and hit each other, Nene would pick up a cast iron skillet, a lamp or whatever she could get her hands on. The strange thing was none of the neighbors knew.

Nene was always the strong willed, impeccably dressed lady on the block. She was petit, 5'1" and probably 120 pounds but she was formidable.

She had quite a few close friends, they all had afternoon drinks before their husbands got home, and they would sit at the kitchen table and drink cocktails and tell stories all day. Sometimes they would go into town to sell some of Nene's dinners. They were all impeccably dressed, and they all had the best manners for the outside world. Everyone admired Nene and her friends.

Nene's friends always treated Renee with kindness and respect, but she did notice Nene would get meaner when she drank all day. As a matter of fact, she would drink every day and the more she drank the more disagreeable she would become. Even Renee's brothers didn't like it when Nene drank. It seems beatings were more likely when Nene drank.

They tried to do everything perfectly or they would get yelled at, or sometimes they would even get a beating with a belt when Nene drank all day. She would have a martini every hour, sometimes she would have them with her friends and sometimes she would have them alone, but she would always have them.

They had to be good in school, they had to get good grades, they had to do chores perfectly and they could not talk back.

They could not speak unless spoken to or interrupt conversations of grown folks. There were a lot of rules, they always tried to comply; they did not want a beating.

Granpa never beat them, he would admonish them if they did something wrong such as a bad grade in school, but he wouldn't yell; he did not have a loud voice, but he got his point across. They were respectful of Granpa, Nene would threaten them with a beating from him after he got home from work, but they feared Nene more than grandpa. Grandpa was mild mannered, and he didn't raise his voice. If it weren't for the nightly visits, he would have been the perfect Granpa.

All the neighbors and family were impressed with Nene and Granpa, it seemed only Aunt China and Renee knew about the fights and arguments. Her brothers always slept through everything and they were always cheerful the next day.

Despite the intermittent turmoil, it was a great year. There didn't seem to be as much violence in America. Her father continued to come to the house on Saturdays to sing with Aunt China. He would sometimes bring other friends who later turned out to be famous singing groups.

Renee and her brothers would watch the Brady Bunch, Bewitched and the Beverly Hillbillies. It felt like things were looking up. She didn't understand why her mother never came over, but she soon learned to do without.

She knew everybody did not have a mother, she was just one of the people who did not have one, she tried not to think about it besides, she had Nene and Aunt China and Daddy.

She even had Granpa although she had mixed feelings about him. Granpa was tall and brown, and he had a funny sense of humor, he was exceptionally good at building anything and he always took the family on trips. He was a great guy, everyone loved him; he was one of the favorites of his family and Nene's family, but Renee had double feelings. There seemed to be two Granpa's. She never forgot the visits at night, she was glad they didn't happen anymore. She hoped they never happened again.

The new worry was Aunt China had a serious boyfriend, what would happened if she got married and left. Would the late-night visits start again?

Renee liked Aunt China's boyfriend; his name was Floyd. He was tall and dark brown with deep dimples on both cheeks and he had a big bright smile and a wonderful laugh.

He was nice, handsome, funny and smart, but she was afraid Aunt China would get married and leave. She couldn't imagine the house without Aunt China, but he did bring a lot of fun and joy into the house. They would turn on the record player and they would dance in the living room; they would watch TV in the living room and Renee was always encouraged to join in. Sometimes they would come up to the room Renee and Aunt China shared when they thought Renee was sleep. They would be in the other bed kissing and it sounded like they were having sex, but she wasn't sure, she would not turn around to let them know she was awake. Renee use to laugh to herself; she knew what they were doing, and they had no clue she was awake.

Then again, she was conflicted; part of her thought they should not be doing that with her in the room. Nene and Granpa were usually out at a function in the lodge when Floyd came upstairs. Sometimes Floyd would come over and so would China's young cousins, they were all in their late teens or early twenties. They would dance and sing to the Beatles and the Supremes and temptations. The house was active and full of life.

Renee enjoyed her friends, family and her pet Foxy. Foxy would always be there but he was always shooed away on previous nightly visits, thank goodness those visits were over.

Aunt China was active in the lodge along with Granpa, she was in the Junior corps of the lodge. China was a majorette baton twirler in High school, and she formed a marching corps in the lodge. She made sure Renee was part of the marching corps. It seemed like half of the kids in Dorsey joined the marching band and Aunt China would have practice every week.

CHAPTER 10
Renee Really Likes the Drum and Bugle Corps, Especially Jerry

Trips to the zoo with Daddy. Mommy has new family.

There was a drum and bugle corps, there were majorettes and flag bearers and dancers, they would march in the lodge parades through the streets of Dorsey.

The crowds would line the streets to see the parade and the marchers loved it. Renee became friends with some of the kids in the marching corps, she even liked one of the boys. His name was Jerry, and he was way older than her, he was 14 which was three years older than her but boy was he cute and cool! He could play drums well; he was tall which was important to Renee and he was brown skinned with big brown eyes and a beautiful white smile. He was friends with everybody, and he was nice to Renee, he always joked with her and he always stopped to talk to her, but she would never tell him how she felt, she was too embarrassed.

Renee always talked to her friends about Jerry, she and her friends always talked about music and boys, those were their favorite topics. She wondered what it would be like to kiss Jerry or even to touch him, she was very embarrassed; she was sure no other 11year old girl had these kinds of feelings. She wondered if her embarrassment had something to do with Granpa. She would keep her feelings to herself, she didn't dare discuss them with anyone. Aunt China guessed she had a crush on Jerry, but she would never say anything, she always kept Renee's confidence. It's a shame Renee couldn't tell Aunt China about Granpa, but he was Aunt China's father, and she would never say or listen to anything bad about him.

During the summer Daddy would take Renee and her brothers to the zoo. He would pile them in his car and off they would go! Daddy loved cars, he would always point out cars and what type they were. He had a Ford, it wasn't expensive like the BMWs, Lincolns or Cadillacs he pointed out, but they thought it was a nice car.

Daddy would explain why the Ford was a great car, it looked good, it was sturdy, mechanically sound and reliable. It would get them to where they needed to go. It was a nice car, and they liked it when he could drive them into the city to the zoo.

They loved the zoo, it was huge; it would take them an entire day to walk around the entire complex. Renee's favorite part of the zoo were the big cats.

She was intrigued with the lions; they seemed to have pent up energy. Lions were King of the jungle; she didn't think they should be cooped up in a cage; they should be in the jungle ruling over all the other animals. It didn't look like they could be king cooped up away from other animals.

The lions roared loud, she didn't think there was an animal in the zoo as loud as them, you could hear them all over the zoo. Maybe that was why they were king of the jungle not to mention they were all muscle, they were fast, they had huge teeth and razor like claws.

Her favorite part of the big cat's tour were the black panthers. The leopards, tigers, jaguars were fascinating to her. They all had their own special traits. Tigers were beautiful and powerful, jaguars were incredibly smart and powerful, the cheetah was the fastest animal, all of them were exquisite, sleek, powerful and deadly.

All the cats were amazing, but she thought the black panthers were probably the most beautiful mysterious animal in the zoo, it was the one instance where black was really and truly considered beautiful by everyone.

Her brothers loved the monkeys, they screamed with laughter at the monkey's antics and even Renee laughed. Daddy laughed along with Renee and her brothers, they all loved the animals and laughter, but Renee did complain about the smell. The zoo smelled like doo do! Is this what the jungle and grasslands smelled like?

Its remarkable how it didn't interfere with her appetite, she was always ready to eat; it's amazing she remained so skinny.

They ate cotton candy, peanuts and hotdogs and popcorn while running through the whole complex, it was always a great day, they loved going to the zoo with Daddy. Daddy would go home to his apartment after a long day at the zoo, they never stayed overnight at Daddy's house but the time they spent with Daddy were memorable moments.

They never went anywhere with Mommy, they really didn't see her except for Christmas; they didn't even see her for their birthdays. They would go over to Nene Boyes house for their birthdays and Nene Boye would always make them a cake and have the Aunts and Uncles and cousins over for a party, but Mommy was never there.

Eventually Renee and her brothers became accustomed to not having a Mommy, but it was ok because they were accustomed to it and they had plenty of family. They had Nene, Aunt China, Daddy, Granpa, and all the cousins plus they had Nene Boye and Aunts and Uncles and cousins on the Boye side of the family.

It seems like Mommy did not have a lot of interaction with her family or Daddy's family, Renee always wondered why.

Renee did hear about Mommy living in a different apartment with a new husband and a new baby. She heard about it through Nene and Aunt China and she also heard about it from Nene Boye and Boye Aunts and Uncles. They never thought she was listening, but she was.

One day Nene and Aunt China said Mommy was coming to their house with Renee's new little Sister. She was curious, excited and nervous. She hadn't seen Mommy in a long time, and it would be nice to see the new baby. Her and her brothers never went to Mommy's house and they never saw her at Nene Boyes house.

One day Mommy came over with the new baby girl and she was adorable. Mommy was tall, thin and glamorous and the baby girl was small, chocolate brown with pretty clothes, she was enchanting.

Mommy greeted Renee and her brothers with a hug and introduced them to their little sister Tonya. Mommy even let Renee hold her new little sister, the boys did not want to hold the baby, they were afraid they would drop her, so they left her in the baby carriage while they played with her.

Baby Tonya played with Renee and her brothers for a while and then Reggie Jr and Little Roy left to go outside to play.

Aunt China suggested Renee take her little sister to the school playground to get some sun and enjoy the warm beautiful day outside. She said Mommy would stay and talk with her and Nene. It was a warm beautiful day and it sounded like a good idea to Renee.

Mommy put baby Tonya in the baby coach, and she showed her where the bottles and pacifier were. Renee strolled her new baby sister to the school playground.

The playground was not as empty as Renee thought it would be. There were classmates there who cooed over the baby girl, they gushed over how cute Tonya was and Renee loved it. It made her feel worldly and important and most of all popular. Even the mean girls exclaimed over the baby.

When they said they didn't know she had a sister, Renee explained she was only a few months old. Renee and Tonya were quite the hit in the park that day and she enjoyed the attention and the sunshine until an hour had passed. She was told by Nene and Aunt China and Mommy she only had an hour with her little sister in the park. She started to head home right away.

When she got back from the park it was time for Mommy and her little sister to leave, when Renee asked when she would see them again Mommy didn't really give an answer. Mommy and Tonya left, and Renee would not see her little sister for years, she would see Mommy at Christmas sometimes, but it was never with her little sister. After some time, Mommy wouldn't even visit at Christmas.

The fact that they never saw Mommy, or her family never seemed to bother Renee's brothers, they seemed to become very accustomed to not having Mommy around. Renee would also have to become accustomed to it or at least act like it.

Whenever she asked why Mommy didn't visit Nene Bobson's or Nene Boyes house she never got a straight answer. She was always told her mother was young or she would visit soon once she got herself settled. Whenever she asked why they didn't go visit she was told her mother's place was too small for a lot of visitors. Renee wouldn't visit her mother for decades.

Renee and her brothers always played in the basement when their cousins came over, they would always make up singing groups and sing songs they heard on the radio. Renee thought they sounded good and sometimes they would sing for the grown-ups upstairs. They always said they weren't bad but of course they were not as good as daddy, Aunt China and some of the groups who came over to visit and sing while they were visiting.

It seemed like everyone in the house sang but Nene, she was always in the kitchen making delicious meals or serving people food. Everybody came to Nene's house to sing and eat, it was common knowledge, that was the place to be. The neighbors never knew about the turmoil in the house in the wee hours of the mornings when Granpa came home from the Lodge. The house could change from the place to be to the place of nightmares. Sometimes Nene would have to go to the doctor's office, only Aunt China and Renee knew the true story.

Nene was a strong successful lady; she had started to sell dinners at bars in town and it was quite lucrative. She always had a savings account and she invested in bonds.

Renee thought Nene put up with violence because all women were treated that way. She didn't know why she thought all women were treated that way; her friends never said their parents acted that way. Maybe she got the idea from TV or the movies. She didn't wonder about divorce; it was not a word used in the Bobson household or any household she knew of.

Renee was twelve now. Her brothers were nine and ten. Aunt China was twenty-one. It was actually a good time. Renee and her brothers would go to places in town, including their other Nene's house. Sometimes they would visit and have fun with cousins and other times they would play with the neighbor kids.

Renee's brothers always looked up to their sister. Nene Bobson was extremely strict with them; they were expected to do well in school, clean up behind themselves, do chores inside and outside and be obedient. Things were ok if they complied with the rules, or so Renee thought.

It was almost 1970 and it was a surprisingly good time for Renee and her brothers, there were still racial tensions but there seemed to be less violence. There was still a war in Vietnam but there was a new President Nixon who promised to end the war.

Maybe he would end it and there would be no more deaths from war. There seemed to still be mean people in school, but Renee seemed to steer clear of them, she was tall, and she was no longer timid, so she was not picked on as much. It seemed bullies picked on people who did not put up much of a fight, Renee refused to be picked on and people in school were noticing.

She got good grades and she had a few good friends, she no longer minded being called on in class and she had a funny sense of humor.

Renee was in a higher grade than her best friend Fawn, but they still hung out after school and on the weekends. They also still went to Basketball and Football games at the city stadium with Fawn's father.

Renee liked Fawn's mother and father. They seemed so normal. Fawn's mom was a teacher who was smart and patient and never seemed angry and her father was a scientist who was smart, kind and wore glasses, he seemed mild mannered. She was surprised he liked sports so much, she didn't think smart, scientific people liked sports.

Renee wondered why her brothers never got to go to the sports events and Aunt China explained how you needed to pay for tickets to go to the events. It was such a nice thing to do, Renee really liked Fawn's parents.

Aunt China was still a champion for Renee and her Brothers, but she didn't have as much free time, a lot of her time was taken up by Floyd. Floyd was great, they sometimes did things together with Renee and her brothers like dance in the living room and watch TV. Floyd was a constant fixture in the Bobson house, he was like part of the family.

Renee was not surprised when Aunt China announced she was going to marry Floyd. She and Floyd were going to live in an apartment in town and she said Renee and her brothers could visit as much as they liked.

Renee was excited for Aunt China and she like the idea of a place to visit but it sure was going to be lonely in the Bobson house without Aunt China. Also, Renee never forgot about the times Granpa came into her room whenever Aunt China wasn't there.

She didn't think it would start again but it made Renee nervous. Her brothers were also sad to think about Aunt China leaving, they always had fun with her. Aunt China was the best ally, she was always protective, fair and fun and comforting to have around.

Foxy also use to keep her company, he was an ally, but he died last year, she missed his friendly face whenever she got home, and she missed playing with him outside and in the house. She also felt safer when he was in the room. She sure missed Foxy; they got another dog, but he was a small Pekinese. It wasn't the same.

CHAPTER 11
Aunt China Gets Married and Divorced

Aunt China and Floyd married. They did not have a wedding. They went to City Hall to get married. Renee wondered why there wasn't a big wedding and Aunt China explained it was too expensive. Renee was shocked, Aunt China always talked about a big wedding and she even looked at magazines with wedding gowns, she was sure she would have a big wedding, but Aunt China was adamant.

It was weird, Granpa had enough money for a new car and boat, she wondered why there was not enough money for a wedding for Aunt China. She guessed weddings must have cost thousands of dollars. They didn't even give Aunt China wedding gifts. She always thought brides were supposed to have weddings and get wedding gifts. She guessed she didn't know much about weddings.

Aunt China was twenty-one. One day she wasn't married and the next day she was. Now she was living in an apartment in town with Uncle Floyd. She still worked at the factory and brought designer clothes home for Renee and Nene.

Aunt China had moved to another apartment with Uncle Floyd and now Renee was in the room by herself, her brothers were in the room next door. Renee didn't like having the whole room to herself and Fawn could not understand why. She thought Renee would be thrilled, she couldn't figure out why she wasn't relieved, Fawn had a room by herself and she loved it. Renee never told Fawn about Granpa's nighttime visits, she was too embarrassed, and she didn't want fawn to dislike her.

Renee became closer to Nene since Aunt China moved out, Renee helped her with her cooking, she learned how to make homemade sausage by grinding up meat and seasoning it. She learned how to make everything fresh and homemade, she even learned how to make homemade wine. They would make the wine and store it in the cellar in a compartment with a door. Renee and her Brothers use to sneak into the compartment and sample the wine, it was good, and you could get quite tipsy with a few sips.

Renee also learned a lot about business, Nene had always taught her and Aunt China there was nothing they could not do. They had to do well in school and save their money for a rainy day.

Renee followed Nene's advice and she did very well in school, she was particularly good in English. She liked to write stories and she did well in grammar and spelling, the teacher always called on her when she raised her hand with an answer to a question. She even had her stories published in school newspapers, she liked to write about things which happened in school and the stories were becoming popular. She was ok in math and science, but she liked English and History. She liked to imagine America and different countries in the "olden days." She daydreamed about stories she heard of her great great grandmother living in log cabins and then working in mansions and the White House.

She pictured the furniture and clothes of people in the log cabins and mansions, she had a vivid imagination.

She knew her ancestors were slaves back then, but she also knew once they were free, they saved every penny and bought up land and built houses. They founded towns where future generations would plant, work, thrive and live. History was fascinating to Renee; she could see similarities in stories of ancestors and present-day family.

Her Brothers didn't care much for English and History in school. Reggie Jr was great at saving, he always had money and refused to spend it; he was a wiz at math, and because he liked science, he got good grades.

Little Roy was not really interested in school, he had a lot of friends and his favorite part of school was recess. He liked running and playing with his friends. He got average grades and Nene always tried to get him to do better but he was more interested in sports and music. Little Roy learned to play piano, guitar and drums at an early age, he even got a drum set for Christmas. Reggie Junior was excellent with money, he would get savings bonds for Christmas. Renee loved reading and writing, she would always get books, journals and pens.

Aunt China lived with her husband now, but she would still bring Renee designer clothes she got at a discount at the factory where she worked. They were all forging their personalities, Nene always knew their strengths and encouraged them to be all that they could be. Little Roy's friends played basketball and football with him while Reggie Jr's friends went on trips with the science club to the creeks and ponds in town. They would look at, collect and research specimens for their science club.

Both Reggie Jr and Little Roy loved battery powered model cars and remote-control model airplanes. They would power them up every weekend when Daddy came to the house and their friends always came over to watch the remote-control plane. They would also make go carts out of crates and wheels and push each other up and down hills of Dorsey.

Renee loved watching the remote airplanes soar high, they always soared pass the treetops and telephone wires and the cars went fast! Renee would practice cheerleading and dance moves with Fawn and other girls from the neighborhood. They would talk about school, dances, TV shows, songs and boys.

Renee was still part of the marching corps but none of the neighbors on her street were members, she guessed they were either too young or too old. Finally, her and her brothers were living a normal childhood or so it seemed.

Aunt China and Uncle Floyd came by to visit every weekend. Sunday was the place to be at Nene's house, she would always have a big Sunday dinner.

Aunt China and Uncle Floyd would be there, Daddy would be there and sometimes Nene's Sisters would be there. Even Uncle Cheeks would stop by sometimes with his wife, Aunt Celia, and daughter Rosy. Rosy would play in the basement with the kids and she would sing with their make-believe singing groups.

Rosy was Renee's age. They were in the same grade. Although they went to a different school, they got along, and they loved to sing together.

Renee always looked forward to the family visits, the house was always spotless and inviting while the family was always warm, funny and loving during these visits. The entire family would visit every month. She especially liked Nene's sisters.

Nene's Sister's looked like her, they were dark cream colored with big brown eyes. Nene's sisters weighed more than her, but they were all about the same height. They were not tall, but they had very loud voices just like Nene. They went from pleasantly plump to obese, their husbands were all thin.

Renee's favorite Sister of Nene's was her great Aunt Sadie, she was cream colored, pleasantly plump with a beautiful smile and dimples. She had perfectly coiffed hair down to her shoulders and she dressed like she was on the cover of a magazine.

She was Nene's age, or she might have been a little older and she was quite pretty. She was kind and attentive and she had a wonderful personality. Before Aunt China was married, Renee and Aunt China loved to visit Aunt Sadie in Philadelphia.

Before Aunt China left home, she and Renee used to visit Aunt Sadie's house monthly, people there were always busy and full of energy.

Aunt Sadie had two Sons Arthur and Darius who were two of Renee and Aunt China's favorite cousins. Arthur and Darius always had lots of friends over. Their house was always crowded with friends of the boys, friends of Aunt Sadie and other family members. Aunt Sadie's husband Uncle Willy sometimes had his friends and brothers over. The house was always busting at the seams with different people.

It was a big three-story house, it was always busy; there was cooking, singing, dancing and loud talking, there were always 20 or 30 people in the house. The Sons played instruments and danced to James Brown and sang R&B songs.

Renee always liked staying over at Aunt Sadie's house, it was an exciting fun place to be and there were never any late-night visits.

The house had three stories, the front door entrance led to a big living room on one side and a big dining room on the other side. The dining room led to a huge kitchen where many of the women gathered and talked and helped Aunt Sadie cook. There were steps which led to the second floor which housed 4 bedrooms and one bath and there were steps which led down to the basement where the children sang and played. The basement also had a bathroom, the kids didn't need to go upstairs to use the bathroom.

Aunt Sadie's house was always a fun, comfortable secure place to be. As a matter of fact, Aunt Sadie had pierced Aunt China's ears in the past and now she pierced Renee's ears. Renee was scared, she was afraid it would hurt but she was excited about being able to wear earrings.

Aunt Sadie thread a needle into a loop of string, she then iced Renee's ear to numb it before she threaded the loop of thread through her ears, it didn't hurt as much as Renee expected. Aunt Sadie reminded her; the loops of string were supposed to remain in her ears for a week.

She was then supposed to put little sterilized broom straws through the holes in her ear and then she could wear small earrings. She felt grown up and fashionable and excited to wear earrings.

One night at Aunt Sadie's, Renee was sound asleep, Aunt China shared a room with her, and she woke up Renee. Renee woke up bleary eyed and she couldn't figure out what Aunt China was saying. Aunt China was pointing at something and Renee looked. There was a big rat on the bed! Renee had seen a mouse on the floor at Aunt Sadie's at night and she didn't like it, but she thought she was safe in bed! She was horrified at the rat on her bed, she wanted to scream but Aunt China stopped her. She and Aunt China put on their clothes and waited outside until the wee hours of the morning for the first bus to come. They left Aunt Sadie's house before anyone woke up without saying goodbye. When Aunt Sadie asked later why the girls left so early, they said they had to get back home early for marching band practice. Whenever they went to Aunt Sadie's in the future they never stayed overnight. It was still a fun place to visit but they never wanted to be there at night.

Aunt Sadie always said Renee spoke like a "little white" girl, Renee didn't quite understand what that meant. She imagined it meant she spoke proper English; Nene didn't like slang or any English except proper English. Renee didn't hear Aunt Sadie use slang, but sometimes her cousins did. She guessed they learned it from school.

At family dinners at Nene's house Granpa would always sing and sip on his whisky and talk with the men, they would all sit around the table and talk about the old days and politics. They seemed to like President Nixon; Renee couldn't quite understand why but they thought he was an OK guy. Maybe it was because all the men were builders and apprentices of architects and developers, they thought Nixon was for the working man.

Sundays were good days for the Bobson's, all the family would get together for a great meal and the house was lively and warm,

Renee always felt great going to school on the next day, Monday. Sunday dinners always put her in a good mood, she always had fond memories of the talk and singing and meals. She always felt like a normal kid after Sunday dinner, she could talk about her family. Even though she never saw her mother and she never really heard about her she was starting to feel like a normal kid.

Renee was afraid to sleep in her room by herself and she had every reason to be wary.

One-night Granpa came in from the lodge and Nene was sleep. Reggie Jr. and Little Roy were asleep, and Renee was asleep in her room. She was awakened by a feeling of something touching her underwear. She was terrified, and she didn't move. She did not turn around to see what it was, but she knew. The touching hands moved from the back to the front of her underwear, and she started to move to make it stop. When she started to move and turn around the touching immediately stopped, and a tall figure quickly left the bedroom. Renee knew who it was, and it filled her with dread. She knew this would not be the end of the nightly visits. She knew she could never tell anyone. She didn't know what to do. Everyone in the house was asleep. Would anyone believe her?

Renee continued in elementary school, she went through fifth and six grades with good grades, she went to sports events with Fawn and her family. She also went on vacations with the entire family, but of course Aunt China no longer went because she was married and living in a different house.

She went to visit Aunt China after school sometimes, they would talk about school, friends and family but Renee never talked about Granpa; she didn't think Aunt China would believe her. She didn't think anyone would believe her.

On weekends Aunt China would come to visit and it was a joyful family reunion, Renee kept Granpa's visits quiet; she never mentioned it, she would usually jerk away when he came into the room.

Renee, Nene, Granpa, and her brothers would go on vacations, sometimes they would go to the family home in Maryland; there was finally indoor plumbing and great movies and concerts in town. Sometimes they would visit relatives in New Jersey, there was Aunt Dodie who was Nene's cousin, and her husband uncle Willy. They had a huge house and land, there would be family members from all over the Northeast and lots of kids. There were acres of land for the kids to play on and Aunt Dodie's house probably had about 8 bedrooms, they always slept over there and there were no nightly visits. It seemed like a normal life for a kid, and it was a nice life except when Renee was home in her room late at night.

CHAPTER 12
Renee Confronts Granpa about Nightly Visits

Granpa seemed to get bolder when Aunt China moved out. He would come into Renee's room every night for about a month, after that he would come into her room once or twice a week. One night, she decided to be bold, she turned around to look at him so he would know she was awake, but he would not stop. She would try to squirm away, and he would continue to touch her. She dreaded nights.

One-night Renee told Granpa how she would yell, and Nene would not like what was happening but Granpa said Nene would never believe it.

She asked how he would explain him being in her room late at night and he said he would tell Nene he was just tucking her in because the covers fell off. Renee would have to keep the nightly visits to herself.

There was nowhere to go and no one to tell, she knew Aunt China wouldn't believe her. She would just need to live with it until she was old enough to move. It's funny how you could be normal and happy during the day and sad and scared at night.

Renee was surprised she could still do well in school after the nightly visits started back up, but they did not happen every night and she was able to decompartmentalize her home life and school life. She kept thinking it would stop and she would get back to a normal life.

She started to wish it were other boys doing what Granpa did. She imagined having a boyfriend to kiss and hold but then she felt guilty. Were these normal feelings or were they feelings girls her age were not supposed to experience?

Her friend Dina had a boyfriend, but she was older than Renee. Renee didn't know about the feelings, but she knew Granpa's visits were wrong. She didn't tell anyone, but she started to wonder what would happen if she told. For now, she would keep it quiet, she didn't want to anger Nene or Aunt China.

Renee was 13 now she was in Junior High in the seventh grade, she was still getting good grades in school and she still had the same best friends, Fawn and Dina.

She even started to make new friends who were usually quiet and more academic like she was. Her two new friends, Molly and Alicia were not in her class, but they were in the same grade and they walked home with her and Dina. Fawn was not yet in Junior High; her mother usually drove her home.

It was funny, even though Dina was different from them they were all very friendly, Dina was one of the popular girls because the boys liked her.

Dina was popular in the classroom, on the playground and in the hallways. She was smart, pretty, athletic and nice. The boys would tease her and talk to her on the way home and Dina loved it, but she would never stop walking with her Renee and her friends.

Renee would never consider herself popular, but she didn't consider herself as a wall flower due to her sense of humor and her friend Dina.

Renee discovered early in life how she could make people laugh. She did not like to laugh at people and hurt their feelings, so she laughed at herself and people usually joined in. She would tell stories of her dog foxy, and her parakeets Sonny & Cher. She would recount how Foxy would get into the homemade wine and act funny and the parakeets would bop to the music of James Brown and Sly and the Family Stone.

She always made people laugh and she could sing, she did not join a choir, she was too embarrassed, but she would always tell jokes and sing in front of a few trusted people.

The mean girls would always pick on Renee, they said she was skinny, tall, and strange looking. They all had boyfriends and they reminded her she would never have a boyfriend. She was the tallest and skinniest in her class maybe they were right. She had super long legs and big breast and a tiny waist, she was tall and skinny. Aunt China and Nene said she had a model's shape, but Renee figured they had to say that. She still liked Jerry in the marching band, and he was still very friendly with her, but their relationship never went farther than friendship.

She dreamed daily and nightly of Jerry kissing her and touching her, but she was too afraid to say anything to anyone. She never even told Jerry, she thought he would be mortified; she was not one of the beautiful popular girls. She had big brown eyes and thin lips; she also had the big, broad Bobson nose!

She did not want to lose his friendship by suggesting anything different, he was good looking and popular and super nice and cool; he was great to have around. She imagined one of the more pretty girls would be his girlfriend.

Her Brothers were in boy scouts and they also went to karate class with their cousins; they were busy, and life seemed very normal.

She and her brothers always went to visit Aunt China, she had a nice apartment and her and Uncle Floyd were always cool. They were not as strict as Nene, they could watch what they wanted on TV, they could eat what they wanted, and they could even go to McDonalds sometimes. It was the best. It was kind of nice to visit Aunt China, she just wished it didn't leave her alone at night.

Aunt China was excited about being married and having a baby, but she had a miscarriage, she started to wonder if she would ever have children, the doctor told her there was something wrong with her uterus.

They didn't know it, but Nene and Aunt China would talk, and Renee would listen. They thought she was out of earshot, but Renee heard their conversations.

They talked about Aunt China and two miscarriages which seemed to have something to do with a biological problem. They talked about Uncle Floyd and Aunt China moving out of Dorsey and into New Jersey so Uncle Floyd could be close to his family and better job opportunities.

Renee hated the possibility of Aunt China being farther away, but Uncle Floyd had a car and he said he would always bring Aunt

China to Dorsey and Granpa could drive them to New Jersey to visit. Aunt China moving to Jersey did have its perks, they lived close to Atlantic City and they could go to the boardwalk and get on the rides when they visited. Aunt China living in New Jersey was not all bad except when Renee was home alone sometimes at night.

Visits to Aunt China were good but there were the nightly visits from Granpa. Renee could also hear arguments between Nene and Granpa, they seemed to happen more, their arguments had nothing to do with Renee, she seemed to hear names of different ladies during those arguments.

As a matter of fact, it seemed like other ladies' names always came up in arguments between Nene and Granpa even when Aunt China lived at home. Aunt China use to commiserate with Nene the next day while Granpa was at work. Renee didn't understand why they were arguing, and she always thought Granpa would never hurt Nene on purpose, but Aunt China knew the whole truth. Nene would talk loudly but Granpa could be violent and physical.

Nene was very pretty, Renee wondered why she put up with Granpa's behavior, but she never got an answer from Nene or Aunt China. At least Aunt China didn't have fights like that with Uncle Floyd; they didn't even have arguments, or so Renee thought.

Renee never saw Aunt China and Uncle Floyd argue, he was always cool and nice to her and she was always cool and nice to him. They would always laugh and joke and kid around together, she thought it was what a successful marriage should look like. Their only sad time was when Aunt China lost the baby, it was a depressing heartbreaking time in their house. When they moved to Jersey it looked like the depressing time had come to an end.

Uncle Floyd drove a truck to different states, and he made a good salary.

Aunt China worked in another factory. They were financially ok thanks to Nene's lectures on working hard for your money and financial security. They had a nice living room and bedroom set, they had new kitchen appliances and they even had a new color TV. They were doing very well for a young couple in their early twenties.

It didn't seem like they had a lot of friends, Aunt China had her family and Uncle Floyd had his family. Aunt China's friends from Dorsey didn't go to see her in New Jersey, it was probably too far.

Uncle Floyd didn't seem to have friends in New Jersey even though he was from New Jersey. Renee thought it was strange how Uncle Floyd didn't have friends, he was a very funny, cool guy. She guessed he was too busy to stay connected to friends, he did drive the truck for days on end across the country. It must have been hard to keep friends under those conditions.

Aunt China came over to Nene Bea's house practically every day, her husband Floyd was never with her, Renee would always be sent out of the room whenever they talked about Uncle Floyd, but Renee could tell there were problems. Renee thought it was the miscarriages, but they had happened months ago. One day Aunt China came to the house and she and Nene forgot Renee was in earshot of them, they were talking about Uncle Floyd and Heroin! He had a heroin habit, and he would spend their money on the drug. He couldn't keep a job because he kept nodding off and Aunt China didn't feel safe anymore.

There were strange people coming in and out of her house all hours of the night and Uncle Floyd told her they were friends. It had only been a year, but Aunt China said the marriage was over and she would need to come back home. The next thing she knew Uncle Floyd signed the divorce papers and Aunt China was divorced and ready to move back to Nene's house.

Nene Bea was sorry the marriage didn't work out, but she understood. She could not bear the thought of one of her children being abused.

Aunt China was divorced and living back home, she and Renee shared a room again and the nightly visits stopped. Aunt China was not going out to have fun, she went to work and came home. Renee was glad the nightly visits stopped but she was sad to see Aunt China so hurt.

Renee continued to get good grades, especially in English and she was learning new subjects. She would now have geometry, trigonometry and second languages. She was in the college prep courses and on the road to a university.

She still had classes with some of the kids in the marching band including Jerry. Jerry was extremely popular with all the kids, he was still cool, hilarious, smart and confident. Renee didn't hang out with him except at band practice at the lodge and classes at school. She never saw him with special girls at school, but she imagined he must have had a lot of girlfriends from out of town. It seemed everybody liked him, and he talked to everybody.

There were still the group of mean girls who bothered her constantly, but she learned to ignore them, she did not let the mean girls or anything else interfere with her good grades. She still had her friends Fawn and Dina.

Fawn was not in Junior High yet, but Dina was. The girls never teased Dina and they didn't tease Renee when Dina was around.

She wondered why they didn't pick on Dina, was it because Dina would tell them off? Dina would never let them talk down to her.

CHAPTER 13
Don't Threaten Renee in School

One day the mean girls were laughing at Renee at the top of the steps in school, they were steep steps, and they were threatening to push her down the steps. Renee shouted, not if I push one of you first as she pushed Gretchen the ring- leader, she watched her tumble down the steps. She asked the other girls if they had anything to say. No one said anything, Gretchen got up, and she made believe she fell down the steps by herself; no one disputed her, and the mean group never teased Renee again, at least not in front of her.

Later Dina told her, "I bet they won't mess with you again" and Dina was right. The mean girls would give her dirty looks when they were together, but no one ever messed with her again.

Renee decided never to let anyone talk down to her again. Nene and Aunt China told her to always stand up for herself and they were right.

Renee was surprised she did not get into trouble at school for pushing Gretchen down the steps.

She guessed no one told the truth, she didn't know if it was because Gretchen threatened everyone because she was embarrassed or if the entire mean girls' team was embarrassed. Nene and Aunt China never found out and she never told them. Besides that, incident, she had a core group of friends in High School, she would never go home with them or hang out with them after school, but they were friendly in school. She even joined the drama club and she helped write plays.

Even Aunt China was in a good mood, she got a job as a secretary in a big company, and she had a new friend named Loraine.

Loraine had milk chocolate skin and an afro that was so big it touched her shoulders. Aunt China had a big afro and Renee even had a big afro, it was all the rage after all it was the early 1970s, Afros and Daishikis were in. Aunt China became more of an activist when she met Loraine. It seemed the times were changing, black people were demanding equal rights and raising fist for black power. Even movies like Shaft portrayed blacks as cool and successful. He was a cool black brother who had an afro, he had beautiful black women and he was a success. Everyone talked about soul power, James Brown had a song called soul power, Marvin Gaye had songs called what's going on and inner-city blues. It was a time of black pride and independence.

Loraine had just divorced, and she had two children under 3, they became common guest at the Bobson's house. Sometimes when Aunt China and Loraine went out on a weekend night Renee would babysit. Loraine always paid her a few dollars, and the kids were great, so she thought this was a great deal.

Dorsey high school only had a sprinkling of black students, but all the students got along well except the sprinkling of mean girls. Mean girls came in all colors, they seemed to all hang together, their only criteria were to pick on anyone who was not in their group. There weren't many Mean girls of color because there weren't that many people of color in the school. Mean girls tended to date or at least sleep with athletes, yet the athletes didn't respect them. They didn't talk nice about the girls out of earshot, they would brag about their conquest.

It seemed this was the only place interracial dating was allowed but the dating did not happen outside of the school grounds. White athletes would never take black mean girl's home.

Renee was friends with some of the athletes in classes. She would ask them why they dated the mean girls if they talked nasty about them.

Renee couldn't understand why they bothered with them, and when she asked, they would say "sex." She understood about sex, but she figured some of the athletes could have any girl they wanted. When she, when she mentioned this the answer was always nice girls didn't put out so fast and they would shrug it off. There was talk of mean girls being easier to sleep with, that was the rumor, but she didn't really know.

The fact is, none of the mean girls bothered Renee after the pushing down the stairs incident but they always found someone else to pick on.

Renee liked high school and she had many people in her classes who were friendly. She had a killer sense of humor and an active imagination; she could always make people laugh. She was not friends with any of them outside of school, but they were friendly in class.

There were a few boys she had crushes on, one was half Asian with big brown eyes, wavy hair and an athletic build. She had daydreams about him and even sometimes at night she dreamed about him, but it never went any farther than the classroom. They teased each other in class but that was the extent of it.

He was honest with her he told her nice things about herself such as her smartness, humor and athleticism. She still marched in the marching band, but she didn't consider herself athletic, but she had a thin athletic build, and she wasn't slow or sluggish.

He also told her she should be more outspoken when people talked to her, but their relationship unfortunately never went any further. She also still had a crush on Jerry, she and Jerry were friendly in school and the marching band, but they never went to each other's houses. They were never more than friends.

In all classes people were friendly and on an equal footing, if the mean girls said something it was from far away. High school seemed cool, students always listened to the music of Elton John, the Rolling Stones, Sly and the Family Stone and other artist. Some of the boys would even bring their instruments to school and play songs for the class. They would sing songs from the Stones and other rock groups.

She wondered why the boys who brought in instruments were never black boys, she guessed the instruments were too expensive.

Most of the time Renee was only one of two or three blacks in the classroom but she didn't mind, she was accustomed to it. The teachers in the Junior High School were much more tuned in to civil rights than the elementary school teachers. Maybe it was the seventies which made the teachers think differently or maybe it was the teachers.

They spoke about equal rights and equal treatment of all students. The lessons they taught in history, English and all her subjects had something to do with current times. They piqued the interest of all the students in their classroom.

Some of the English teachers even examined the lyrics of some of the pop songs on the charts which talked about equality and justice. It might have been the Vietnam War which awakened the teacher's awareness, or it could have been the Nixon Presidency. Nixon's politics was dividing the country. Renee thought it was a good thing he was ending Vietnam and he did seem to have a relationship with China. In 1972 he even got a Panda from China, wasn't that supposed to be a diplomatic achievement? Maybe Nixon wouldn't be so bad after all.

Renee was accustomed to interacting with white people. There were white people across the street in the house she grew up in, there were white people in school and there were white people in every store she went to. The seventies were a time for better relationships among black and whites or at least that's what Renee thought.

She started to read about a group called the black panthers, they talked about unjust police treatment and unjust treatment in jobs and housing, but Renee thought all the hatred and division had ended. She thought differently when she started reading about Angela Davis and Huey Newton. They seemed smart, educated and civic minded but she didn't think they would affect the people across the country and the schools like Dorsey PA. She didn't think Dorsey PA had a problem.

No one complained about the treatment of blacks in Dorsey, sure most of them had blue collar jobs but isn't that because that's what they wanted to do? After she started reading about the black panthers she realized, she had never had a black teacher, which seemed strange.

She knew a lot of black factory workers or labor workers who were smart as or smarter than most of the teachers who taught her, but they never became teachers. She wasn't sure if it were because they couldn't afford college or if they were just overlooked. Some of her neighbors went to college but they were still blue-collar workers.

Every black person she knew were all blue-collared workers except her mother's brother who was a doctor. He seemed to be the exception to the rule. Renee wondered about unjust treatment of blacks and she wondered if the Black Panther ideology would reach the high school.

It seemed as if the ideology entered the school slowly but surely. There was suddenly, an uncomfortable thickness of anger and distrust in the air in high school and she wondered if her High School in Dorsey PA would ever be the same. It seemed like one minute everyone was friends and the next minute there were race riots in the school.

The surprising thing was there were race riots in a school where there were not many black kids, it looked like the black kids refused to be bullied any more even if they were only 1/10 of the population.

There were daily fights with chains and baseball bats, and there were even rumors of a few knives, she couldn't understand how this happened in her school.

Thankfully, no one was hospitalized or killed but it was loud, scary and confusing. Renee hoped they weren't returning to the 1960s. There were no race riots in the schools in the 1960s but there were riots in some cities.

Most of the people still got along in school but it seemed the mean girls had new targets, they now hated people of color; there were no longer people of color in the mean girl group. Were they fanning the flames of hatred?

There was racial tension, but most students still got along if they did not agree with the Black Panthers. They were not popular in school, students who spoke about equal rights were usually targets in the race riots. Luckily, the race riots usually happened after school or on the weekend, it looked like the school administrators stopped violence on school grounds during school hours.

Renee wondered if students of color would have gone to jail if they were found disrupting the school schedule or destroying property, she wondered if white students would have gone to jail for the same offense. In any case it looked like the school stopped it, she could not remember riots from the past which interrupted a school day.

School continued and the race riots eventually stopped, all races continued to get along but there was always an undercurrent of differences and mistrust with some students. Maybe that's why Renee didn't really stick out in the high school, she was different but so were a lot of other students. Unlike elementary school, different people were not ostracized if you didn't rock the boat.

Nene Bea had a family gathering at her house in the summer one day and everybody was there. All of Nene's Sister's and their husbands and all her children including Aunt China and her friend Loraine and her kids.

Daddy was there and so was Uncle Cheeks and his wife Celia and Cousin Rosy. As usual the kids were going to go into the basement to sing and play and Renee noticed there was another teenage girl with Uncle Cheeks, her name was Augusta.

She was Renee's age which meant she was a year older than Uncle Cheeks daughter Rosy. When she asked her who she was Uncle Cheeks let her know it was her cousin, it was uncle Cheeks daughter. Aunt Celia didn't say anything she treated Augusta like her own child. Augusta was now part of the basement singing group. She did not live with Uncle Cheeks and Aunt Celia, but she came over every year after that. Renee wondered if there were any other unknown cousins in the family. She thought of ancestors such as her great grandmother's mother who were slaves, they managed to stay together but did other slaves have babies taken? Did they grow up not knowing their family?

Renee and her brothers heard stories of Mommy having another baby with her husband Carl two years after she had Tonya, but Mommy didn't come to visit again, and they never were told where she lived.

They never visited Mommy and neither side of the family talked about her.

Daddy still visited on the weekends and he would sometimes bring girlfriends, the first girlfriend Renee remembered was Mary. Mary was short and curvy with full lips, dimples and a wide smile. Her hair was done in a flip and she had an infectious wide smile. Renee thought she was pretty; she must have been Daddy's age. She worked as hairdresser and she lived in the city like Daddy. Renee thought she sort of looked like Aretha Franklin, but she didn't sing.

Mary came over with Daddy for a few years, practically every weekend, Renee liked having her around. She was a good listener and always easy to talk to. She could talk to her about school and her brothers and practically anything, but of course she never talked to her about the nighttime visits that happened in the past. That subject was still embarrassing and scary, she still didn't tell anyone about the visits. Who would believe her? She was certain no one in the family would believe her.

Aunt China was still living at home and still friends with Loraine. They would go out every weekend Renee would babysit. Occasionally they would meet men they liked, and the men would sometimes come to family functions, but they would never last long.

Reggie Jr and Little Roy slept in the bedroom next door and Loraine's children slept in Aunt China's bed while the two women were out. Renee liked having them there, there were never nightly visits when someone else was in the other bed.

Loraine's kids were fun and sweet natured they always listened, and they rarely cried. They only needed a coloring book and a few toys, Nene always fed them before they came upstairs.

Things were rather good, Renee was getting good grades in school; she loved writing and she got A's in English, French, Spanish and history. She even got a B in Math she was in 9th grade and she loved all the subjects.

 She got along with most people at school although she was only friends with them in classes and on the school grounds, she never took home friends from school.

She joined drama clubs, she even helped write some of the plays and she wrote in the school newspaper. Things were really looking up.

CHAPTER 14
Aunt China Meets Someone Great

This time there's a nice wedding!

Aunt China met someone when she went out with Loraine, he played piano at one of the clubs, his name was Carl. He was shorter than the men Aunt China usually liked, and he was chubbier, but he had a nice face and nice wavy hair. He also worked as a clerk for the IRS, it was considered a good job with good benefits. He was 10 years older than Aunt China, but he was quiet and serious yet affable. He and Aunt China went to the club he played in every weekend and he came to the house to visit Aunt China at least every week. He was always serious and thoughtful to Renee and her brothers. He always had time to listen to them and talk to them.

Aunt China and Lorraine were best friends, they talked on the phone every day, but they didn't go out as much.

Lorraine was talking to her husband again and Aunt China was with Carl, they would double date sometimes. Lorraine would rarely bring the kids over to spend the night, but Renee didn't worry. Everything was going to be alright.

She assumed she was much too old for nightly visits, she was after all in ninth grade, she was going to be fifteen; also, Granpa always went out on weekends and sometimes he didn't come home until Sunday nights.

He was always exhausted, he argued with Nene and then he went to bed because he had to get up to go to work the next morning.

The arguments between Nene and Granpa were loud when he got home on Sunday nights, but he never stopped the weekend explorations outside of the home. Renee and her brothers and Aunt China didn't even mention it, they were quite accustomed to it the arguments, they had gone on for years and they knew Granpa would never leave. The fact that Granpa would never leave for good, comforted Aunt China and her brothers but it left her with mixed feelings.

Renee wasn't afraid of nightly visits because she thought she was too old now, and Granpa was usually gone nights and weekends but she began to worry when Aunt China and Carl became close.

She wondered if Aunt China would marry again, it was only a little over a year since her divorce, but she was getting serious about Carl. He always came over and he and Aunt China even took her to watch him play piano at the club. It was a wonderful on those nights; the singers were great, and Carl really could play the piano. It was surprising, Aunt China never sang with him.

Nene and Granpa also liked Carl, he was quiet, thoughtful and a good provider, and he also loved Nene's cooking.

She would make his favorite dishes whenever he came over, and he would declare it was the best food he had ever eaten, he became part of the family.

Carl came to family barbecues and Christmas, it seemed like they saw him more than Granpa. Granpa was always at work in the morning and the family was in bed if he came home at night. They didn't see him on weekends except sometimes on Sunday. The entire family would watch TV like nothing had changed. They were fun evenings with funny TV shows like all in the family, the Jefferson's and good times.

Renee wondered if all families were like that. Did all men in all families act like that? Did they only come home some nights and stay away on weekends? Carl didn't seem to act like that.

Carl talked about his mother and father, his sisters and brothers, and his nieces and nephews. His family seemed different than theirs but then again people on the outside thought their family was ordinary and normal. Everyone who came to visit loved the good times at their home, Renee's family seemed loving, warm and fun. Granpa was always there for family gatherings.

Daddy and his girlfriend were always there, the only one who wasn't there for family gatherings was mommy. She was never at this house or the Boyes family gathering.

At a family gathering barbecue in the summer, Carl and Aunt China announced their engagement. Everyone expected it and the entire family was excited, even Renee was excited, there was going to be a wedding this time.

The Barbecue lasted all day and into the night. The family played card games and dice games, they sang and danced and eat.

There were spareribs, burgers, hotdogs and chicken; Granpa manned the grill with the meat. Nene made all the side dishes, she made collard greens, macaroni and cheese, potato salad, macaroni salad and homemade baked beans. As usual, the food was delicious; people had 2 and 3 servings.

Not only was family there but neighbors from her street, and friends from blocks away came to the barbecue. Renee's friend Fawn and Dina came with their brothers and Sisters and their Mothers even came. It was the party of the year and it wasn't even the Wedding or Reception.

Aunt China and Nene would plan the wedding soon, they were thinking of having the reception at the lodge. Aunt China had grown up as a Junior member, she had marched and become a majorette and she had gotten the town children involved. The lodge always had fond memories for her, it was a home away from home plus they had nice parties; they could decorate it for a wedding reception. It would be perfect.

Nene and Aunt China made plans for the wedding in the Methodist Church in Dorsey. Renee wondered why the wedding wasn't in the Methodist church where Papa Boye was the pastor.

Renee and her brothers never went to the church where Papa Boye was pastor. She didn't think Nene Boye went to Papas church either.

She wondered if any of her mother's brothers and sisters went to his church. Maybe it was too far? It wasn't in Dorsey, but everybody had cars; she couldn't understand why they never went there. When she asked Nene and Aunt China, they said they didn't know why her Mom's family didn't go there but for them the Dorsey Methodist church was closer.

Granpa was at the "lodge" most weekends and they usually didn't see him until Sunday, but he always had projects around the house he would tackle when he came home. He would put up paneling, drop ceilings, and sunken living rooms.

He completed a lot of projects for the house and the lodge to make sure Aunt China had a nice place for her after her wedding reception and the celebrations before the wedding.

Renee and her friends and brothers cleaned the lodge and made favors for the wedding. Aunt China bought wedding invitations and she and Nene addressed them while Renee and her brothers sealed them and put them into piles for mailing. They had an assembly line going at the dining room table.

Nene, Aunt China and her friends decorated the lodge with streamers and wedding bells and just married signs. The lodge staff which was headed by Granpa set the tables up with white tablecloths and crystal glasses. The place was beautiful for the wedding, they were all excited about it, they couldn't believe it was going to take place on the next day.

Aunt China and Carl would live together in an apartment in the next town over. Carl would become Uncle Carl, but Renee already felt like he was her Uncle. He was already part of the family.

Aunt China would no longer live in the house, but she told Renee she could take the bus and visit any time.

She told her she could even bring Fawn and Dina; they were cool girls, and they would all have fun together.

Renee and Aunt China went to bed in their room, it would be the last night Aunt China slept there; they both dreamed of a big, beautiful wedding which would happen the next day.

IT'S ABOUT TIME

It was finally the day of the wedding, and the Bobson house was busy. Ladies and girls were putting on make-up and getting their hair done and men and boys were trying on tuxes and straightening ties and bow ties.

Aunt China's best friend Loraine looked wonderful in a yellow A line gown, she was ready for the wedding and she helped Aunt China with her makeup, hair and gown.

Nene wore a grey gown, it was beautiful; it had short sleeves, and a cinched waist, it really highlighted her figure. Nene was around 48 and she didn't look a day past 35. She had no wrinkles; no extra fat and her hair were perfectly coiffed. She looked like a vision in grey satin.

Renee wore a blue A-line gown with a bow in the back. Her hair was in a flip and she even wore lipstick! Granpa was tall and handsome in his grey tux and tie and her brothers, who were now 11 and 12 looked handsome in their black tuxes and bow ties. They were all waiting for Aunt China to come downstairs.

Aunt China came down the stairs in a stunning white A-line gown with a lace collar and lace sleeves. It showed off her perfect figure, like Nene she had ample cleavage, a small waist and a long torso, she wore a beautiful lace veil which flowed down to the floor.

Lorraine held her veil as she came downstairs, Aunt China held her dress up and she walked gracefully down each step. She was breathtaking everyone in the house gasped.

It was 3 o'clock and the limo arrived, Aunt China and Loraine got into the Limo, Renee and her Brothers and Nene rode with Granpa. They all arrived at the church early for the 4 o'clock wedding, this gave Aunt China time to apply last minute fixes before walking down the aisle. Renee was not in the wedding party, Aunt China only had a Maid of Honor and Carl only had a best man, the Bobson family sat in the pews.

Carl got to the church along with his best man and he looked excited yet nervous. He was looking down the aisle waiting for Aunt China.

The church was packed as they sat and waited for the bride.

There was a stillness and gasp from the guest in the church when Aunt China appeared in the doorway. She walked down the aisle with Granpa, they were both beaming.

Aunt China looked radiant in her white gown and veil and Granpa looked dashing in his tux. The groom looked on from the altar with proud excitement as Aunt China walked down the aisle. It was a solemn, hopeful day filled with expectations, new beginnings and hopeful blessings.

After the ceremony, the bride and groom greeted everyone in the church line with thanks and gratitude, they were met outside the church with attendees waiting with rice and streamers. It was a wonderful, bright sunny day; the trees were in bloom and the temperature seemed exactly right. It was probably 78-80 degrees; it didn't seem too hot or too cold. It was a perfect summer's day.

Everyone one drove to the Lodge for the reception, it had transformed from a party venue to a wedding reception showplace. There was a round horseshoe shaped altar adorned with flowers where the bride and groom could greet guest. The bride and groom had not arrived yet, they were taking pictures first at outdoor sites. There were cards with the bride and groom names, candles, flowers and pictures on each adorned white table.

There was a special table with chairs decorated especially for the bride and groom. There was exquisite china and crystal.

This table was for the bride, groom, maid of honor, and best man. It was a day Renee would never forget; it was a magical time.

There was always a bar at the lodge, it was serving drinks, and to adults who attended, it was cocktail hour: time for drinks and hors-d'oeuvres. When the cocktail hour was over people sat at their tables just in time to see the bride, groom, maid of honor and best man arrive. The bride and groom danced the first dance to Stevie Wonder's "You Are the Sunshine of My Life." Afterwards Aunt China danced with Granpa, and Carl danced with his mother. Everyone got up to dance and dinner was announced. After the song ended everyone went to their tables for the dinner hour.

Dinner choices were steak, chicken or Fish, Nene had cooked all the sides and provided fresh meat, she wanted everything fresh for the wedding, the food was delicious, Nene even let Renee have a little Champagne to toast the bride and groom.

The night was full of delicious food, dancing and celebration; everyone at the wedding had a ball at the gala of the year. It would be talked about for decades, the Bobson's were the talk of the town and considered the cream of society.

The event was ending, and Aunt China and her new husband Uncle Carl had changed clothes. Aunt China had changed into a lovely blue dress which had designs of different shades of blue and Uncle Carl had changed into a blue suit. They said goodbye to all their guest, they hugged Nene, Granpa. Renee and her brothers before they left. They left in a powder blue Cadillac with just married signs on the car.

They were going to the airport to go to the island of Jamaica! Renee could not wait to get married, she daydreamed of her wedding day and wondered who she would marry, and she daydreamed about boys. None of the boys she knew from school or from the neighborhood seemed like marriage material.

She liked Jerry from the marching band, but she knew he was only a friend, he would never marry her. She probably would have to leave home to meet someone to marry.

Renee, Granpa and her brothers had to clean up the food from the wedding. They had to clear off the tables and they had to help pack up the left-over food. People from the lodge would clean the place but they had to take the decorations off the tables and collect salvageable things that could be taken home. There was not as much food left as Renee thought, they would take home mostly decorations on the table.

They all got home late; they were exhausted. They put the leftover food up and they would put the decorations up the next day, the decorations were still in boxes. The wedding was fun, but it was a lot of work. Renee slept like a baby that night.

Aunt China's wedding was the talk of Dorsey, the next day was Sunday and they were going to Church the church was no longer decorated for a wedding, but it was beautiful with stained glass windows and velvet seats. The ladies talked about how beautiful the wedding was and how good the food was, the men talked about how great the lodge was; even the kids talked about how much fun it was.

After church Renee talked on the stoop with her friends Fawn and Dina. They talked about the wedding, but they also talked about music and their favorite songs and dances, they were determined to be singers and marry singers. Dina and Fawn knew boys they liked but they did not have boyfriends, Dina had broken up with her boyfriend and Fawn's crush never became her boyfriend.

Renee had the same problem with Jerry. It never seemed to go anywhere. They liked the boys they talked about, but they really would rather marry singers, they imagined they would have glamorous lives married to singers.

They talked about the beautiful bridal gown and what their gowns would look like. Their gowns would be like Aunt China's except maybe more satin, lace and hoop skirts. They talked about their wedding party, they of course would have many more bridesmaids and grooms' men. They all agreed Nene would oversee the food.

They talked about husbands who would make a lot of money and be madly in love with their wives, their children would be beautiful, smart and obedient. They were all ready for marriage and children.

They walked around the streets of Dorsey pointing out boys that might make good husbands if they never got to marry singers. Renee always played along but she knew she could never marry any of the Dorsey boys.

Most of the boys did not think of her that way, the boys who acted like they might like her were not attractive to her. They were either too chubby or too nerdy looking.

She could think of two boys who might have liked her, Denny had a nice face and dimples and a great brown complexion, a nice smile and personality but he was too chubby, and he was shorter than her. It was a shame because he was a funny, nice guy.

Alvin was tall, and he was a creamy caramel color, with dark brown eyes and wavy hair. He was brilliant, he got straight A's all through school and he always talked to her even outside of school. Aunt China always tried to get her to talk to Alvin since 6 grade, but Renee always thought he was too nerdy. He was ok looking, but he wore thick big glasses, she was not attracted to him. Both Alvin and Denny remained friends with her throughout school, but she never could seem to get farther than friendship with neither of them.

CHAPTER 15
Life Back to Normal

The beat goes on.

The summer before tenth grade, Aunt China was married and the house seemed quieter. Nene still had afternoon cocktails with her friends and Granpa sometimes did not come home after work and he was not there on Saturdays; he would complete projects on the house and sleep at home on Sundays. This became a normal occurrence in the Bobson household.

Nene continued to use her kitchen to make and sell her dinners, she even sold them in bars and restaurants, she saved the extra money and she always encouraged Renee and her brothers to save their money so they would not have to depend on anyone.

Fawn had a crush on Kenny, she liked him since the sixth grade, but he never noticed her. She went to his games and cheered him on and tried to talk to her, but he ignored her.

She never gave up on him, she figured she was not going to marry a movie star and Kenny was the next best thing. She was determined to get his attention. She would be going into high school after the summer. She and Renee would be in the same school.

They could go to Kenny's games together and Renee would see Jerry at the games, he was leader of the school band, maybe things would change.

Dina had a new boyfriend; he was in the cool group; all the girls liked him even though he wasn't into athletics or any other clubs. The girls liked him because he was good looking, smooth and self-assured. Renee thought he was ok, but she didn't know what all the fuss was about, he looked OK, but she didn't see anything special about him. He wasn't super nice, or super good looking or super smart.

Aunt China and Uncle Carl continued to come to the Bobson house every Sunday for Sunday dinner. Uncle Carl would talk about his job at the IRS, he would talk about all the phone calls and paperwork and he would talk about the club where he played piano on the weekends. Aunt China would talk about her job in the factory where she worked for years, she still got major discounts on clothes and she still bought Renee some of the newest designer styles; they could have never afforded them if they bought them in the stores.

Sometime Aunt China came to the house by herself if she had the day off from work, she would take the bus and visit with Nene. She didn't complain about being married like she did with her first marriage, and she couldn't wait to have kids. She liked to visit with Nene.

Aunt China never drank alcohol at home or Nene's house, she would have a drink at the lodge or when she went to clubs but never more than one or two drinks. She never drank with Nene.

She and Nene both smoked since she could remember, they would smoke together but they would never drink together. Uncle Carl never drank at Nene's house neither, as a matter of fact, Renee didn't think Uncle Carl drank at the club. Aunt China and Uncle Carl would drink soda at the house.

Granpa would drink at the house on Sunday's but it was only one or 2 drinks of Bourbon or whisky. It looks like Nene was the only one in the house who had drinks all day. There were always cocktails with her friends, sometimes they would finish off a pint of vodka in a day.

At times Nene would get mean and Aunt China or Renee would try to substitute soda for the cocktail, but she would get meaner, and they would stop talking about it, no one usually said anything because it never changed the outcome.

Aunt China still led the drum and bugle corps on the weekends and Jerry was still a member. The holiday parades were still a vital part of Dorsey culture.

There were parades in the summer such as the Labor Day parade but there was never a Thanksgiving Day parade, Renee and her brothers would bundle up and go into the city to see the Thanksgiving parade. The TV stations televised it, but it was always better to go in person.

It was always cold, but it was worth it, there was nothing better than a parade with different marching bands, floats, baton twirlers and dancers. The parades in the city were even better than the Dorsey parades, no matter how cold it was there were always thousands of people. It was better than the Dorsey parade, but those parades were also crowd pleasers.

The Dorsey parades were exciting and entertaining, the entire town showed up to see the activities. Renee always felt proud marching to the beat of the drums, she wasn't shy about marching in front of the town; this is probably why she wasn't shy about joining clubs at the school. She liked the discipline and uniformity.

Out of all the clubs she joined, the Drama club was her favorite, she was surprisingly good at it and the people in the drama club were like her. Strangely enough people in the drama club were not the most popular kids but they had no problem performing in front of the entire school. Perhaps they didn't mind because they could be different characters.

Renee also joined student government, she was always class President for homeroom, and students always liked her sense of humor and good ideas for her class. The idea which got her the title of class President was 5 minutes of power down time before the next class. The students seemed to like that idea and it took off. Renee was never one of the popular girls, but she was becoming known and liked among the students in school.

It looked like it was going to be a good year in 10th grade. The subjects were harder, and Fawn and Dina were not in any of the clubs she was in, but it was going to be a good year. Things were not bad at home or in school, life was really looking up for Renee. She had her neighborhood friends she hung out with after school, and on the weekends, Aunt China didn't live there but the nightly visits had stopped, and her brothers hung out with their friends in the Neighborhood.

It was great to be fourteen, she would be fifteen this year, and the bad days were over. She was rather good at writing, maybe she would go to college and get a job as an executive secretary. Even

Nene told her she was smart, and she could have any job she wanted, the future looked bright to Renee.

There were not a lot of people in the executive secretary jobs that looked like Renee, but she was sure she was smart as most people and would be able to get a great job. Maybe she would even get a job in the DMV or banks! Her Brothers were also rather good in school, they would probably go to college and get a good job too.

Her Brothers would probably get a city or state job, like working at a college or water works or even a sanitation worker, those jobs paid well and had great benefits. The future was looking bright for all of them.

Her neighbor's parents all had decent jobs. Her next-door neighbor Mr. Houston worked as a coach in one of the schools, his wife did not work, their kids use to walk everyone to school. Most of their neighbors had decent jobs, Fawn's parents were teachers, and they were the only black teachers she knew. Other neighbors worked in the bank, construction companies and local government buildings as cleaners, postal workers or clerks.

Nene Boyes neighborhood was different, her kids were teachers, doctors and architects but the people in their neighborhood were factory workers, construction workers and mechanics. The houses cost less on that street, yet the neighborhood seemed much more inviting. There was a corner store owner on Nene Boyes street, all the kids use to hang out there and there was never any trouble, it was a place to meet after school for a soda, candy or chips.

The corner store was there from the 1950s, it was the place to meet, the granddaughter even went to school with Renee. Her name was Marcy and she probably was the richest girl in the school, but she was never a mean girl, she was smart and fun, and she had friends of all races. Renee wondered if she wasn't a mean girl because her skin was dark. She was the color of dark chocolate with a great thin shape, a big bright smile and curly hair. She didn't straighten her hair like a lot of colored people, she never tried to hide her race or ethnicity.

She was popular with all the students, but she was more popular with black students. Marcy preferred being called black, especially after James Brown came out with the song, "say it loud, I'm black and I'm proud."

No one ever reacted when she corrected them, she was not a loudmouth or troublemaker; she quietly spoke her feelings without fear or anger. Renee admired her, she was just a regular person, she was a cheerleader with some of the mean girls, but she never hung out with them and they never talked bad about her. She was invited to all the parties and she would even invite Renee to parties her parents threw for her on her birthday or other holidays. Her parties were the only parties Renee was invited to except for parties thrown by her neighbors.

Renee was starting to feel popular; she still wasn't part of the mean girl group, but she was part of the drama group. She was also invited to class political groups and she got along with Marcy' friends. She was beginning to be a part of quite a few groups in school.

Aunt China and Nene were quite pleased with how Renee was doing in school, she no longer seemed to be an outcast; she was going to parties and friends called her from school. Aunt China even tried to continue her quest for her to hook up with Alvin, he called her sometimes, but she could only see him as a friend. It was too bad Jerry never called her at home. Even her brothers got calls from friends, they would always go over their friend's house, but they were not going to parties; they were too young, they were only 11 and 12.

Renee didn't hang out at her friend Dina's house; Dina was always at her boyfriend's house; she was never home. The only other houses she hung out in were Nene Boye's and Fawn's house. Even in Fawn's house, she usually stayed on the front steps or the back yard. She rarely went into the house and Fawn rarely went inside Renee's house.

Nene Bobson still had her cocktails and she still had arguments with Granpa on weekends, but she was more encouraging to Renee and her Brothers. She kept reminding them of going to college and being trailblazers, she set the example by selling her dinners in bars and restaurants and saving the money in a separate bank account.

She always told them how everyone should have their own bank account. She made them start Christmas clubs and savings accounts and they could check their passbook and make deposits whenever they wanted. They would save their birthday money, Christmas money or money from chores and odd and end jobs in the neighborhood. They always had the full amount in their Christmas Accounts which was $50, and they always had a little money in their saving accounts. They even saved money in a coffee can for extras like albums, comic books and bike parts.

They had saved extra coffee can money, and Renee and her brothers had saved $20 for the year. It was enough money to go see James Brown in the Big dome in the city!

They asked Aunt China if she would take them and she agreed. They would go see James Brown on a Saturday when she did not have to work. Uncle Carl would not be going because he had to play the piano on Saturday nights at the club. It was an exciting time, they would be going to see James Brown the Godfather of Soul, she wondered if he would sing "I feel good" and "say it loud, I'm black and I'm proud." It was going to be their first concert, Aunt China said there would be thousands of people and it would be fantastic music, they couldn't wait.

They had enough money for the big day although Nene reminded them not to spend any of their money if they wanted to go to the concert. Nene would not allow them to take money out of their savings account. She was adamant about having money in the bank for a rainy day.

Renee and her brothers always had different amounts in their coffee can. Reggie Junior always had the most money, he didn't spend his money unless it was a necessity. Renee would spend her money on albums and comic books, but she would save some, she didn't like being broke.

CHAPTER 16
We Must Save Our Money

Do we have enough for the James Brown concert?

Little Roy would spend his money as soon as he got it, he never had more than a few dollars in his coffee can. He would have the most comic books, albums, candy and the latest gadgets like transistor radios. He would go to the ten-cent movie more than Little Reggie and Renee. He liked going to the movies with his friends. Little Roy always said, "You must have fun now, who knows what tomorrow would bring."

Nene would allow it, but she would remind all of them if you spent all your money, you won't have money if you want to do something special? When it was time to plan to see James Brown, they found out little Roy didn't have $20 he didn't even have $10. Nene found out when they all had to count their money for the big day.

Aunt China figured they would need money for the bus to the city, they would need money for the concert tickets, and they would need money for food and souvenirs. She figured it would be $20 or more, Renee and Reggie Jr had $20, and they could do odd jobs to make another $10 but it would be hard for Little

Roy to come up with $25 or $30 in another month even if he cut lawns and did odd and end jobs. The concert was in April 1973 which was only a month away.

Renee was 14 she would be 15 at the end of the year, she would be in high school next year. She babysat to make money, she cleaned up a ladies' house and took care of her two children for the day and she got $10 for 1 day of work.

The woman was pleased, her house was clean, and her children were clean, they weren't hungry, and they were laughing and playing. The woman told Renee she would call her every week!

Renee now had $30, and she might even have $50 by next month in time for the concert.

Nene told Renee she couldn't understand how Renee got such glowing reports about cleaning a house when she didn't even clean her own house.

Renee told Nene she felt sorry for the woman and kids, the kids were living in filth and they were dirty. She cleaned up the house and kids so they would be comfortable.

Nene's house was always spotless, Renee and her brothers had chores and kept it clean except for the messy closets and drawers. Nene would yell at Renee for hiding dirty underwear before laundry day and Renee could never explain why she hid them. She would put her underwear in the washer herself but sometimes Nene would go through her drawers, both Nene and Aunt China said it was a bad habit, Renee agreed.

Renee learned to wash her underwear by hand, she didn't want to disappoint Nene and Aunt China.

She also told Nene she cleaned the woman's house and children to make money for the concert, plus she brought Nene French fries from McDonald's which she loved. Nene certainly understood about making and saving money.

Reggie Junior and Little Roy mowed lawns, trimmed hedges and cleaned out garages to make extra money for the concert the following month. They made an extra $30 each! Added to the money they had in the coffee they would have plenty for the concert.

All of them knew they had to use money in the coffee can, Nene would never let them use money in their saving account, they could look at the savings books to make sure their money was still there, but they could never take it out without first asking Nene, her name was on the account along with their names. She told them a concert was a good thing they would remember, but they could save separately for that by doing odd jobs.

Even when they did odd jobs, they had to put $5 in their savings account and the rest they could put in the coffee can or spend. Their savings accounts were increasing.

Renee's coffee can had over $40, she had taken $5 every week for albums and comic books, but she never let it get to less than $30. She wanted enough for great food and souvenirs at the concert.

Reggie Jr had almost $75 in his coffee can he rarely bought comic books or albums, he would read Little Roy's comic books or go to the library. If he wanted to listen to music, he would listen to the transistor he got for Christmas or he would go downstairs and listen to the record player. He rarely bought candy or things to eat, he always waited to eat whatever was in the house. He always had the most money in his coffee can.

Roy Jr always had the least amount of money in his coffee can, if Nene didn't control the savings account, he would not have any saved money. Roy Jr would work hard and make the money, but he would practically spend all of it the same day. He did not have enough money in the coffee can go to the concert yet, but he figured he would get it before the concert next month.

He brought all his favorite comic books, he had McDonalds, candy and cookies every day. He was living it up, it was a great time. He always had a great time. He would save for the concert later, he wished Renee and Reggie Jr would stop bugging him about it.

The week of the concert finally came, Aunt China and Nene made Renee and her Brothers count their money to make sure they had enough for the big day. Aunt China wanted to be sure everyone had at least $25, they would need that for bus, concert, souvenirs and food.

Renee had exactly $25, she spent some of her money, but she knew she needed $25 for the concert. She wanted to get a program and a T-shirt for a souvenir.

Reggie Jr had almost $50! He always let his money build up. He had spent a little on a remodeled model airplane that ran with a remote, but he liked to keep most of his money. He wanted that airplane for a long time and he finally got it, even the kids in the neighborhood and Renee, Daddy and Nene loved it. It went pass the treetops and it went fast. He was glad he could get the model plane and still have a lot of his money left. He could spend $25 on the concert and still have money left. Maybe he could spend less on the concert. He might like a T-shirt if it looked nice, but he didn't care about a program and he wouldn't eat unless he was hungry. He probably wouldn't need to spend the entire $25.

Little Roy only had $10! He and Reggie had the same odd jobs and made the same money, where did his money go? Little Roy couldn't figure it out, he thought he would have more time to save. He was really starting to panic, Nene wouldn't budge, he could not use his saving account; she said he had enough time to save his money just like his sister and brother. Aunt China had come over and she said $10 would not be enough for the ticket and bus fare. He would not have money for food or souvenirs.

They all had school and they needed to concentrate on homework after school, they could not do odd jobs before the concert this weekend. Odd jobs were normally done on the weekend. They could do no more odd jobs before the concert. There was no way Little Roy could make extra money. He couldn't believe this was happening. Was he going to miss the concert?

Nene would not budge. She was strict when it came to managing money and schoolwork. He couldn't think of a way to make more money and Nene told Aunt China not to chip in any money, she said this would be a great lesson. Renee and Little Reggie wished they could at least have given little Roy a few dollars for bus fare and food. Aunt China was trying to figure out how she could still take little Roy to the concert.

The day before the concert Aunt China begged Nene to let little Roy go, she could loan him $5 for bus fare and a hotdog; she did not want him to miss the concert, it was a once in a lifetime opportunity,

Nene finally agreed to allow Aunt China to loan little Roy $5 and no more. He would have money for concert tickets, bus fare and a hot dog. He would not be able to get souvenirs, he didn't have the money. He would need to pay Aunt China back by taking the bus to her apartment and helping her clean out her closets and junk drawers.

It wasn't a job Little Roy looked forward to, Aunt China's apartment was big, and Nene wouldn't let Renee and Reggie help him. She had lots of closets to clean out, she said he could help her clean out old shoes, bags and clothes. They would put the old things in bags for donations and have the church come pick everything up.

The junk drawers were all junk mail and old magazines and newspapers, they would throw all that stuff away in big bags and they would take the big bag to the dumpster.

It was a lot of work for $5 but at least he would have enough money to add to the coffee to reach $15, he would have liked a souvenir, but he didn't have enough money. As a matter of fact, maybe Aunt China would give him $10, Nene said no but Aunt China might give him more for helping her clean without telling Nene.

He wouldn't get the money before the big day tomorrow, but he might have a little money left after the concert. There was a batman comic book and a baseball and bat set he wanted to buy, he really wanted to get it and he hoped Aunt China would help.

Friday night they all took baths and got ready for the James brown concert which would take place the next day. They had their clothes laid out and the money they needed for the big day.

Nene had given Renee a coin purse to put her money in and she gave her brothers a little wallet. They couldn't wait until tomorrow.

No one could sleep Friday night, it seemed like Saturday morning took forever to get here. It was finally Saturday, this afternoon they would take the bus to the city with Aunt China to see the concert.

Aunt China was already here, she didn't usually arrive this early on a Saturday, but she decided to have breakfast with Nene, Renee and the kids. Uncle Carl was not at the house, he liked to sleep late on Saturdays. Nene could not see wasting money on a James Brown concert, but she did like seeing Aunt China and the kids so excited.

Granpa was home, he did not go to the lodge yet today, but he was not downstairs for breakfast, he had gotten home late from work and the lodge the night before and he slept in.

They were going to take the 2:00 p.m. bus to the city, they would get there around 3:00, and then they needed to take a subway to the concert dome, which might take another half hour. Once they got to the area of the concert dome they could walk around and window shop before the concert.

There were toy stores, clothes stores and even a pet shop near the concert dome, there would be plenty to do if they got there too early. Aunt China wanted to get there early in case the concert was crowded with a long line. She wanted to make sure they could get into their seats in time to see the entire show which started at 6.

They had a big breakfast of pancakes, bacon and eggs and grapefruit halves with sugar sprinkled on each half, it was Renee's favorite breakfast, and it was also Aunt China and her Brother's favorite breakfast. Nene had everyone's favorite, she wanted them to get a good breakfast, and she didn't want them to be hungry in the city.

After breakfast Renee cleaned up the dishes and the kitchen which was one of her chores, and she went upstairs to put her clothes on for the exciting trip for the afternoon. Her Brothers had cut the lawn and hedges which was one of their chores. They all had lots of chores, which included cleaning the house.

Renee's chores were inside the house and her brothers had to clean and landscape the outside. They had finished their chores and were putting on clothes for the big day.

They were dressed and ready to walk with Aunt China to the bus terminal, she did not drive; she took the bus everywhere unless someone drove her. She gathered them all and they left the house to start the walk.

It was a chilly day in April, they all had on long sleeves and pants. They wore light jackets, and they were quite comfortable, it was a brisk day, but the fast walk and excitement kept them warm.

They walked to the bus terminal which was only 10 minutes away and they were talking excitedly about the James Brown concert and the big city. Aunt China had been there before and she told them about the stores, the pet shop and the street vendors who sold soft pretzels for 10 cents on the corner. She said soft pretzels with mustard were delicious, they did not want to leave the city without tasting a soft pretzel.

They were on the bus talking excitedly about the upcoming events and Aunt China had to laughingly tell them to speak softly. They were making so much noise the other passengers were staring at them.

She spoke softly as she told them about the time, she was a kid riding on the bus. She had to sit in the back of the bus because black people had to sit in the back. After that Aunt China never sat at the back of the bus, she always sat in the front. She told them at least she didn't have to sit in the back of the school bus when she was a kid because she walked to school.

Renee had heard about black people who had to sit at the back of the bus, but it was still almost unbelievable to her. She couldn't imagine giving up her seat to another person unless they were elderly, pregnant or handicapped.

She wondered what she would have done if someone her age demanded she give her seat up because they were a different color. Aunt China said that's how it was, you could go to jail for not giving up your seat.

They were all silent for the last 5 minutes of the bus ride, even her brothers seemed to understand how some people were treated differently than others.

The bus arrived at the Philadelphia terminal, and they had been riding an hour. They had passed lots of neighborhoods with children playing on big lawns, they passed neighborhoods with apartment buildings and row houses, they passed lots of schools, factories and stores. Some of the stores were corner stores, some were big stores which took up most of the block. There were big stores in Dorsey like the A&P and the toy store but these stores on the bus route were way bigger.

The bus stopped a little after 3:00 p.m. and Aunt China reminded them, they needed to take a subway downtown to the dome concert hall.

Renee wished they could have stayed longer before they took the subway, there were so many busy, bustling people and stores on every block. She would have loved to go and look in each one of those stores, but they needed to catch the subway 2 blocks away.

The walked quickly to the subway and they were surprised to see it was an underground train, Aunt China didn't tell them that! It looked like there were thousands of people running down the steps to get subway tickets and rushing through turnstiles to wait for the subway train.

Aunt China got tickets for all of them at the subway ticket window and she gave Renee and her brothers their tickets which were coins called tokens. They put their coins in the turnstile and waited on the platform for the subway train.

Renee didn't want to get too close to the edge of the platform, she was afraid someone might push her, or she might accidentally trip and fall. Her Brothers were playing but they didn't get too close to the edge, Aunt China made sure of that.

They were all looking down into the tunnel to see if their train was coming but the train was the number 1 train, they were waiting for the number 3 train.

People crowded on the number 1 and number 2 trains and Renee wondered if they would get a seat on the number 3 train. The trains that came before her train were really crowded.

She saw through the windows of the trains that came before and she noticed people standing up and holding on to bars above their heads. She asked Aunt China if they would have to stand up for the entire ride and Aunt China said they may have to stand up because the trains were crowded. She told Renee and her brothers if the train were crowded, they would need to grab the hangers above, or the bars below, she would help them; she assured them they wouldn't fall.

Finally, the number 3 train came, and Aunt China grabbed her brothers and told her to follow her and hurry up. They ran on the train and saw people rushing off, there were 4 vacate seats, they grabbed the seats quickly. People piled onto the train and all the seats were full in a minute, other people had to stand up and hold on to the bars for the ride. It was going to be a 15-minute ride, she was glad they got seats. There was nothing to look at, the subway tunnel was dark; all they could see were lit signs at each subway stop and crowds of people waiting.

They had been riding about ten minutes and Aunt China told them to get ready, the next stop was their stop, and they would have to quickly get off the train. The train stopped at the next station, Aunt China, Renee and her brothers quickly ran to the doors to get off the train. There were so many people, Renee was relieved they got off without getting lost in the crowd.

CHAPTER 17
We're in the City for the James Brown Concert!

They walked off the train and onto the platform and they found they would have to walk up the steps to get to the street. When they got up the steps, there were signs all over pointing to different streets, Renee was amazed Aunt China knew which signs to follow. They followed the signs to 40th street and they went outside. There were stores everywhere, there were hotdog vendors and hot pretzel vendors and ice-cream vendors. They couldn't wait to sample some of the vendor goodies.

It was their first time in the city. Who knew when they would get to go to the city again? Renee wanted a hot pretzel. Aunt China said it was delicious and Renee couldn't wait to try one. It was 50 cents, and she would still have money for everything else.

Little Roy wanted both—a pretzel and ice cream. He would still have enough for everything but souvenirs and a program, he would rather have the pretzel and ice-cream. Everyone was amazed at how thin Renee and her brothers were, they ate a lot. Little Roy got an ice cream with sprinkles and nuts and syrup and Aunt China held his hot pretzel. He said the ice-cream was the best he'd ever had, he loved to eat sweets and goodies.

Reggie Junior wasn't hungry, but he had never had a soft pretzel and he wanted to try one, so he bought the pretzel and added mustard. It was as good as Aunt China said, it was warm, soft, chewy and spicy, it was delicious.

Aunt China got a soft pretzel also. They were eating their goodies and they were stopping at the stores to window shop. There were adult sized dolls in the windows called mannequins, they were dressed in glamorous clothes with matching purses and shoes. Renee hoped they could come back and go to the stores, but they kept walking.

They had finished eating their goodies and they came to a gigantic toy store, the window had mannequins which looked like children playing with toys and it was only four o'clock, so they had time to go into the store to look around.

They went into the big toy store and there was a train set that included an entire village, there were toy people in the village and toy houses. The train track rode through the entire village, it made a whistling sound and blew smoke. There were Rock em Sock em Robots which her brother had and there were dolls which Renee use to have. There were easy bake ovens and tiny kitchen sets and tiny supermarket sets, there were three floors and they visited all of them.

They left the toy store, and it was already five o'clock. They passed more clothing stores and they went in one for a few minutes, but Aunt China wanted to show them the pet store before they got to the concert dome. She told them they didn't want to come to the city without seeing the pet store.

They continued to walk and finally came to the pet store. It was huge, the window had stuffed puppies on one side and stuffed kittens on the other side. There was a display of mannequin children on the floor playing with the stuffed puppies and kittens. They all went into the store and were met with the sounds of puppies yipping, kittens mewing, and birds chirping but their first stop were the puppies.

There were puppies in cages, Renee felt bad, she wondered if they ever got out, but they seemed to be happy they were yipping and wagging their tales when they came close to them. There were 2 or 3 puppies per cage, they were all different colors and breeds; they were excited, and they licked her hand through the bars of the cage.

They walked further into the store and passed bird cages, there were singing parakeets on perches, they didn't fly they sat on their perch; there were 2 parakeets per cage, the birds turned their heads to look at them, they seemed curious.

They finally came to the kitten cages, they stretched on forever; their cages went from one end of the store to the other end of the store. The kittens were running and rolling over each other and they were licking each other; Aunt China explained it was the way kittens cleaned each other.

Renee and her brothers could have watched the kittens and puppies all day. There were also adult cats and dogs, but they seemed less active and excited.

Renee was glad when it was time to leave the pet store, she enjoyed looking at the animals, but she felt bad knowing they had to stay there for the night. She asked Aunt China what would happen if no one bought them and she was told they had to stay there until someone bought them. She explained the kittens and puppies were always the first to go, they didn't stay in the store for long. The older pets usually went to older people, younger families usually liked kittens and puppies.

Renee asked Aunt China if she and Uncle Carl were going to get a cat or dog, but Aunt China said they didn't want to leave a dog or cat home by himself all day while they were at work. She said they wouldn't have time to get up early before work to walk it and they didn't always come straight home from work, it wouldn't be fair to a cat or dog.

Aunt China looked at her watch and it was already 5:30, the concert would start in half hour; it was close, but she wanted to hurry and get there to get their seats; she could see a line from down the street. They quickly walked to the concert hall and waited on the line. There was a long line, but a lady who was from the Dome asked if anyone already had tickets. When Aunt China raised her hand and said they had tickets, the lady told them there was another line for them, and it was shorter. Thank goodness Aunt China had already gotten tickets, that ticket line only took them 10 minutes to get through.

They went inside the concert hall and it was huge. There were marble ceilings, velvet ropes and draperies as soon as they walked in. There was a man standing behind velvet ropes who collected half of their tickets and gave them the other half; he pointed to one of many doors in the center.

When they got to their door which said section C it led to a section with what looked like hundreds of seats. They entered at the very top of Section C and they needed to get to row 113, they had to go all the way down near the front; it was dark, and they could barely see the numbers or letters.

When they finally got to their row it was only a few rows from the front of the stage, it was in the middle of the row and they had to step over people to get to their seats. Once they got to their seat, they had an excellent view of the stage, they could see the emcee talking on the stage and they could hear him perfectly. Aunt China had gotten them excellent seats, they weren't going to miss a minute of the show.

They had already stopped to get pretzels so they weren't hungry, the show was 2 hours, and they would get food later it they got hungry, they would get souvenirs after the show.

The Emcee was telling funny jokes about people from his neighborhood, and he was imitating different acts. He would soon be introducing the first act; two acts would perform before James Brown.

It was a night packed with stars, the emcee introduced Cornelius Brothers and Sister Rose, they sang a song Renee never heard and the crowd cheered. Renee heard of the second song they sang "Its Too Late to Turn Back Now." The crowd got out of their seat and danced. Aunt China, Renee, and her brothers also got out of their seats and clapped but they were anxious to see James Brown.

The emcee came on again after the Cornelius Brothers and Sister Rose left the stage, Renee noticed a lot of people were coming to find their seats or leaving to get food, she was glad they didn't have to leave their seats.

The emcee introduced the next act, the Staple Singers; they sang Respect yourself and the crowd was on its feet and singing along. When they sang, "I'll take you there" the crowd went wild.

Aunt China and Renee danced and clapped and went crazy, they knew all the words to the song. They had forgotten about James Brown for a moment.

Renee noticed a strong odor in the concert hall, she knew it was pot because she had smelled it before in school when the "cool kids" smoked it on the school grounds. The odor was so strong because a joint was being passed down the aisle where they were sitting. They passed it to her, and she passed it to Little Roy who was sitting next to her. She told him to give it to Aunt China, but he went to puff on the cigarette and Aunt China snatched it from him. Aunt China gave it to the person who was sitting next to Reggie Junior and told them to pass it on.

It looked like pot was going around the entire concert hall, no wonder everybody was dancing. It was a party atmosphere, everyone was clapping, singing and dancing. People were screaming laughter at the Emcee and everybody was in their seats screaming for James Brown to come out.

An hour had passed, and Renee wanted to go to the bathroom before James Brown came on, she didn't want to miss a second of the show.

Aunt China took her and her brothers to the bathroom and to get a hot dog, they all had enough money for a hotdog and soda, they quickly went back to their seats, it was delicious! As soon as they sat down and finished their hotdogs it was time for James Brown.

It was the moment they had all been waiting for. The crowd was on its feet screaming.

James Browns band came on stage first, they played an electric instrumental song called "Make It Funky." The crowd was on its feet dancing to the music and screaming for James Brown when suddenly he appeared. The crowd went wild, one of the band members said, "What you going to play now?" James Brown said, "Whatever you're going to play, it's got to be funky." He then went into the song "Make It Funky."

He was sliding across the stage, twirling around and doing splits. It was electrifying, and the audience danced and screamed in their seats and up and down the aisles. The crowd didn't even try to contain themselves. He then started singing "In a Cold Sweat," "I Feel Good" and the crowd was singing along. He never stopped, he danced, twirled, he did splits, and he slid across the stage the entire time.

He only slowed down with a song called "It's a Man's World" and you could hear a pin drop in the concert hall. The audience was swaying to the music and waving lighters, they were mesmerized. It was a thought-provoking song, the dancing stopped but the audience never stopped singing along with the song. The music picked back up and he was singing "Soul Power." The audience was singing along and dancing when finally, he broke out in song and started singing "Say it loud! I'm black and proud!" The entire audience was screaming the song, this was the James Brown and the black community's anthem.

It was hard to believe it was 9:00 p.m. The concert was supposed to end at nine, but it was not over. James Brown started singing "Please, Please, Please" into the mic and the crowd went wild again. He grabbed the mic. He was glistening and pleading, "Baby, please don't go." He screamed, "Baby, you did me wrong. Baby, please don't go," and he fell to his knees. One of the band members rushed over to put a cape on him, while helping him up and assisting him in walking off the stage.

James Brown shrugged off the cape, twirled around, and made his way back to the mic to scream "please, please, please, baby, please don't go," and the crowd was besides themselves.

He shrugged off his cape and walked back to the mike for three more times to scream "please, please, please" for ten minutes. He finally walked off the stage and the concert was over; it was time to leave.

The crowd waited to see if there was going to be a second encore but there wasn't. The concert was over, and they were glistening with sweat!

Renee and her Brothers walked to the lobby with Aunt China, the lobby was mobbed. There were long lines everywhere for programs, T-shirts, eight-track tapes and all kinds of merchandise. Renee got a T-shirt and a program. She wanted to remember the night forever.

Reggie Jr. got a t-shirt, but little Roy didn't have money for a T-shirt or program. Aunt China got him a program and told him and Renee and Reggie Jr. not to tell Nene. They vowed not to tell her; Little Roy put his program in his inside coat pocket.

They needed to take the subway and the bus back home and they were walking down the streets in the city singing James Brown songs. It seemed like everyone in the city was walking down the street singing James Brown songs.

They took the subway home where there was standing room only and everyone on the subway was singing James Brown songs. People were singing and dancing up and down the subway aisles, it was an exciting memorable night.

They finally got off the subway to catch the bus, the bus was quieter; there was no dancing or singing on the bus, it looked like the concert people did not get on the bus.

As a matter of fact, there were more people of color on the streets of the city and in the subways. There were people of color on the bus but not as many as in the city. The closer they got to Dorsey the less diverse it became and there was no singing and dancing. They were back in Dorsey, but the excitement of the evening had not worn off.

They walked the ten minutes back to their house before Aunt China left to go home, she had to take the bus back after she walked with them.

It was after 11:00 p.m. by the time they got home but Nene was still up. She asked everyone how the concert was, and they all talked excitedly, even Aunt China talked enthusiastically before she left.

The kids talked about the Staple Singers singing "I'll Take You There." Nene liked that song, she had the record. They talked about James brown singing "Say It Loud" and she also liked that song, Nene was very civic minded. She always talked about the rights of black people, she even marched in some of the civil rights marches including marches with MLK.

They talked about James Brown doing the cape act with the song "please, please, please" and Nene laughed. Everybody was in a good mood that night, Granpa was already home and in bed and Renee and her brothers went to bed. The next day was Sunday but they probably wouldn't go to church, they usually only went on special days. They sometimes went to church if the church had a special activity or trip but going to church was not a weekly activity.

Everyone slept soundly that night, the next day was a usual Sunday of breakfast, TV and playing outside with friends. Granpa had gone to the lodge at lunch time, Nene had drinks with friends at the house and Renee and her brothers toured the town to tell people about the concert and show off the newest dance moves and sing the latest James Brown songs.

April was a great month; they had just gone to a concert and next week was Easter!

They always got a separate Easter basket with jellybeans, marshmallow peeps, and chocolate foil wrapped Easter baskets. They would go to church on Easter, but they didn't really talk about religion at home. It's strange they didn't talk about religion, Nene could quote the Bible, she knew a lot about it, but she didn't always go to church, on Easter she didn't go with Renee and her Brothers, they would usually get their Easter Baskets after church.

April continued into May. Soon it would be summer. Visits to Aunt China's house were always enjoyable. She also liked hanging out with friends on their stoops. Of course, her favorite thing was going to the park or candy store with neighbors and friends.

Even school was enjoyable, classes came easy to Renee and she enjoyed the kids in her classes and the teachers. She didn't get into trouble at home, she knew how to stay away when Nene was drinking and so did her Brothers; they could tell when Nene was not in a good mood. If you crossed Nene, you would get a beating with the leather belt. They did not like the beatings, sometimes they left welts on their skin.

The nightly visits hadn't happened in ages, Renee was sleeping well, and life was surprisingly good, but then again; all good things must come to an end.

Renee and her brothers noticed how Granpa came home every weekend now, he would come home late 12:00 am to 1:00 am and everybody would be sleep. He and Nene didn't even argue about it anymore, he came home late, fixed the house, watched TV and went out every night and every weekend at about 6:00 or 7:00 p.m. after dinner. Everybody had gotten use to Granpa's schedule, they would all be asleep when he arrived home.

CHAPTER 18
Why Is Granpa Doing This?

One Saturday night Renee was awakened by something touching her underwear, she was half asleep and thought it might have been the dog Pecky, Foxy had died years ago now there was a new little dog named Pecky. Renee turned her head and notice Granpa standing over her with his hand on her panties. He put his finger to his lips and motioned for her to be quiet and Renee jerked away and rolled to the other side of the bed. She quickly jumped over the bed railing and ran into the bathroom, she stayed there for an hour scared to death.

She was three years old again. She didn't know what to do, should she tell Nene? She didn't think that would be a good idea, she didn't know if she would believe her. She had asked her brothers in the past if they got any late-night visits and they always said no. Should she tell Aunt China? She didn't think so, Aunt China always spoke about Granpa like he was a Prince.

Renee knew she couldn't tell Aunt China; she would never believe her. She finally came out of the bathroom an hour later and hoped that it would never happen again.

She was almost fifteen. This could not be happening! Granpa was in his fifties, why was he doing this? She was filled with terror, shame and dread. Did she do something wrong? Why does he feel he can do this? She never dressed provocatively; she was never alone with him. She couldn't understand why it was happening, she didn't have any great curves, she was tall and skinny, it wasn't like she was curvy and irresistible. She hoped her reaction would stop it once and for all. Maybe her reaction frightened him off, she certainly hoped so.

The next day was Sunday, Renee didn't say anything at breakfast and neither did Granpa. He acted like it was a normal Sunday, he ate his breakfast read the paper and watched TV before going to the lodge.

Renee acted like everything was normal also, she ate her breakfast but this time instead of hanging out with Fawn or Dina she walked around Dorsey by herself.

She didn't go to church that Sunday, but she started to wonder what God thought, she went to her room and opened the Bible, she had a hard time concentrating but she knew God was there and would always protect her. She felt nervous and scared and shameful, but she knew God still loved her and he would never leave. She read that in the Bible.

The next night was Sunday night and Renee was awakened again, it was déjà vu. There was a hand on her pants and inside her pants! Renee finally said she was going to tell Nene and Aunt China and Granpa said they would never believe her! He had a tight hold on her with his hand over her mouth. She tried to get up and run but Granpa held her down, when he uncovered her mouth she started to yell; he quickly got up and went into his bedroom where Nene was sleep.

Renee went into the bathroom to lock the door and to think. She realized it was time to tell Nene and Aunt China, she was terrified! She would tell Nene in the morning before she went to school. Maybe Nene would make it stop, she didn't like wrongdoing; she was very opinionated at she always chastised people about bad behavior, Granpa wouldn't be there before school, and it would be before Nene started drinking.

She was shaking she was so nervous, maybe she should be quiet and just keep running away from Granpa, he would probably get tired or bored eventually. The problem was Renee didn't think he would stop, and she could not stop thinking about how shameful and wrong it was. Maybe if she told Nene in the morning it would all be taken care of when she got home from school tomorrow afternoon. Nene would make him stop and everything would go back to normal; or at least she hoped so.

It was Monday morning and Renee, and her Brothers went down to breakfast, they always ate before school; Nene said they needed full stomachs to concentrate and do well. Renee's brothers had left, and she asked Nene if she could speak to her for a minute before school. Nene said sure, she could always talk to Nene.

Renee told Nene how Granpa was coming into her room and touching her, and Nene was horrified, Renee thought she would faint. She told Renee don't worry, she would take care of everything and it would never happen again. Nene thanked her for telling her and she said she should never worry about telling Nene about anyone who hurt her no matter who it was. Nene told her to go to school and not to worry, it would all be straightened out when she got home, she would never need to worry about nightly visits again.

Renee did feel better, she was glad to finally get everything out in the open, Nene said she would tell Granpa to never do that again.

She had a rather good day in school although she was still a little worried about what would happen when she got home.

School was over for the day and Renee and her Brothers were treated as if nothing had happened, Nene assured Renee things would change and she would be safe and protected.

They watched TV that night, Granpa was not home from the lodge when they went to bed, it was a great night.

The next morning Nene was quieter, she sent Renee and her brothers to school as soon as they ate; Renee didn't get the chance to speak to Nene before school that day. The entire week was the same, they really did not get a chance to talk to Nene before school and they didn't get a chance to talk to her after school, Nene usually had cocktails with her friends when they got home from school, they never talked to her about anything serious in front of her friends.

Renee figured Nene must have said something to Granpa because the nightly visits stopped. He always got home late, and he went straight to bed when he got home, and he always went to work before everyone got up in the morning. Renee felt a sense of relief, everything was back to normal there was no difference in the house.

Saturday morning was a bright Sunny day in May and Renee went down for breakfast, her brothers were still sleep and she could talk with Nene to make sure everything was ok. She said good morning and she thanked Nene for listening to her, she said she was going to eat and start her chores for the day. Nene asked her to explain again what Granpa did, and Renee explained it. Nene asked if Renee could have mistaken it for tucking her in and Renee said no, she reminded Nene how he said no one would believe her. Renee didn't even mention all the other times, she only mentioned the last time.

Nene said there was a misunderstanding and she believed Granpa. Renee said she didn't misunderstand and then she did tell her it wasn't the first time. Nene said she was lying and was hot in the pants and sick in the head. Nene had already called Aunt China to tell her about the lies Renee was telling and Aunt China was going to come right over.

Renee was horrified, Granpa was right, no one believed her, she should have shut up and just ran. Why did she have to tell what happened? Everybody was going to hate her, she wished it would all just go away, she would hate it if Aunt China were against her; she was her biggest ally and protector.

Aunt China came over and Nene told her what really happened in Granpa's words. "Renee had kicked the covers off, and Granpa covered her back up" that's all that happened. Aunt China asked what the problem was, and Nene said Renee accused Granpa of touching her through her panties and molesting her.

Nene told Aunt China how Renee was a liar and "too hot for her pants" Renee didn't even know what that meant, her friends didn't use that phrase and no one around the house used that phrase.

Aunt China and Nene were furious with Renee, they told her if she didn't stop spreading lies about Granpa they would send her away to a military school or a home for girls. They said Renee was obviously crazy and needed a psychiatrist. They were pointing at her and pushing her, it scared her because they were all at the top of the steps and they were furious; Renee thought they were going to push her down the steps.

She just stood there silently; she didn't know what to say; they would never believe her. They finally got tired and went downstairs. Renee went into her room to grab her Bible and she went into the basement, she didn't know what else to do, she just started reading. She couldn't really concentrate but she read something about the meek inheriting the earth. She didn't want to inherit the Earth, she just wanted to be OK.

They called Daddy and they told him to come to the house. Renee was terrified of what Daddy would think and she was right, they told him about the accusation. Daddy asked her why she would say such a thing and she told him it was the truth, but he didn't believe her. Daddy avoided her after that until she was an adult.

She guessed they never called Mommy and she didn't know how to contact her; she was glad she didn't know how; she was embarrassed. She wondered what Mommy would do, she probably wouldn't believe her either. Mommy didn't really visit, and she never saw her after that until she was an adult, the closest she could get to Mommy was a visit to Nene and Papa Boye and Mommy was never there.

She would still visit Nene and papa Boye she would never say anything to them or that side of the family, she was too embarrassed, and she knew no one would believe her,

Granpa certainly had one thing right, no one believed her, Granpa knew what he was talking about, he said no one would believe her and no one did. She didn't dare tell any of her friends or anyone else, thank goodness her brothers didn't know; they were always sent away when the discussion was about Granpa. Everybody in the family acted like they hated Renee, she wished she didn't say anything; she wondered if she could have stopped it without saying anything.

A few days after she told Nene, Renee was on punishment for lying about Granpa. She could not watch TV, go outside or speak unless spoken to but she could go downstairs to get meals and water. The family didn't speak to her and she was not to say anything. She wondered how long the silent treatment and punishment would last.

Not long after the incident, in the middle of doing her homework in the evening, she went downstairs from her room to get a glass of water and Granpa followed her downstairs. He said to her "you could tell that, but you couldn't talk about not finishing your chores." Renee went back upstairs, she didn't dare say anything else, at least there were no more late-night visits.

She finished her homework and went to sleep and had horrible nightmares about hands grabbing her in the night.

She had to get it together, she had school the next day. She couldn't let anyone in school know there was a problem, they would laugh at her and think she was crazy. She wondered if 10th grade next year would be the same. She was still on punishment, she couldn't watch TV or go outside with friends; she could only sit on the steps in the house and read her Bible, it seemed like no one bothered her when she sat on the steps to read her Bible. The steps were near the living room and TV, but she could not see the TV. She could sit there but she couldn't see the TV from the steps.

It was ok to read the Bible that was the closest she could be to any family members. This behavior continued until the end of the school year; she would be in 10th grade next year. It was probably going to be a rough summer.

Nene and Aunt China only told her brothers Renee was on punishment for lying and not doing her chores. They never explained what she was lying about, and when her brothers asked her, she said it was about chores.

Her Brothers thought that punishment was fair, and Renee never told them anything different. Not even Granpa bothered her when she sat on the steps to read her Bible, it seemed to give her peace and comfort and it was acceptable to the family. Granpa didn't bother her about anything, sometimes Nene would be mean and call her a crazy liar and Granpa would tell her not to be mean, he would remind her Renee had a problem.

It was strange, the bad nightmares were getting worse, someone was always chasing her and trying to kill her, she was scared to go to sleep but, in the daytime, she was always most comfortable in her room by herself. Her room felt like a sanctuary now that she was sure no one would bother her there, if only she didn't have nightmares.

CHAPTER 19
Granpa Was Right: No One Believed Her

At least school was normal.

At least Renee was treated normally in school, she could be a normal person; she was still in drama and she wrote for the school newspaper. She also kept an A average; she was particularly good at English and math.

She loved to write, she could write about different places and people and she could write about happy endings.

She liked Math, it was exact, the answer was based on facts and they never changed, she understood Math.

Even Nene and Aunt China eventually softened up, nightly visits were never spoken of again and they were proud of her grades and her being published in the school newspaper and drama club.

The town thought Renee was a good student, people bragged to Nene about how proud she must be, and Nene always agreed.

Events which happened in the Bobson house stayed in the Bobson house.

Renee wondered if all families were like her family, other families seemed to be normal, loving and warm but then again Renee's family seemed to be all those things. She wondered if her friends had any problems like she had. She didn't think so. She didn't think other families had the town fooled like her family, people would be shocked.

She couldn't wait to leave Dorsey, she wanted to see the world, she had gotten through tenth grade and now she was in eleventh grade. Next year was going to be a long year but at least there would be the Prom and Graduation.

Everybody in town thought they were a normal healthy family, Granpa went to work every day and he was a respected great builder and Nene had a catering business in town. Aunt China was hard working and happily married, her husband was successful, and they had a nice apartment. Her brothers were good boys at home and school, they were in clubs and they had paper routes.

They even thought Renee was perfect. She was shy, but she was good in school and destined for great things.

Renee learned things aren't always what they seem. She learned to go with the flow and act like everything was normal, she didn't complain, and she didn't dare bring up the past.

The summer continued like any other summer. The past was not mentioned, and Renee talked about her Senior Year in High School.

One day Aunt China brought a group of young women home, she said Uncle Carl was their manager; they performed at the club and they were an excellent act. They sang popular songs and did stand-up comedy, Renee wished she could see them at the club; they were lively and hilarious!

They ranged in ages sixteen to thirty; they were beautiful, chatty, entertaining women. They always dressed beautifully, and their hair and makeup was immaculate, it shocked Renee when Aunt China and Nene told her they were transvestites, they were born boys, but they didn't tell people.

Renee couldn't believe it; they certainly didn't look like boys or men. She wondered why no one could talk about it, they were some of the funniest, smartest, most authentic people she knew. She liked them more than most people she met, and she had a lot in common with the youngest of the group. The youngest was only sixteen. Her name was Shena, and she use to play jacks with her. She was caramel colored with a slender build, she wore her hair in a ponytail.

They sat on the front steps and played games and listened to music. They became friends but Renee never mentioned nightly visits, she saw how people reacted and she didn't want Shena to react that way.

Shena didn't mind sharing private information with Renee, her life sounded sad, her family refused to see her, it seemed the only happiness she had was performing with the rest of the group. The group became her family, her true family kicked her out, she hadn't seen them in three years; she was thirteen when she was kicked out! It was amazing, she was so upbeat and hopeful; No one could have guessed her story.

Renee could understand being kicked out of a family, all you had to do is say one wrong word. Sometimes you didn't even need to say anything.

When she talked to Shena, she realized this was another group of people who were mistreated, Shena told her how she was spit on; beat up and called names; she didn't like discussing genders. Renee could understand why she didn't want to discuss it, but she wondered if things would ever change.

The group was never around when she hung out with Fawn and Dina, they were usually around in the evenings; Nene usually fixed their favorite meals. No one outside of the house ever talked about the group, maybe they didn't know about them; Renee never mentioned them; Nene and Aunt China said everyone would not understand.

It was hot that summer. The temperature was in the high eighties for three days in a row. Renee, Fawn, and Dina were sitting on the stoop; they talked about a big party the Houstons were having. All the neighborhood teenagers would be going, it was the talk of the town. Fawn was only fifteen, and she was not allowed to go, she was going to a basketball game with her dad. Dina was seventeen and she was going; she was also going to get a new dress. Renee was also seventeen. Nene was strict about parties, but she could go because the Houstons lived next door and they knew her since she was a baby.

She didn't need new clothes; Aunt China still brought her name brand clothes from the factory and they fit her perfectly. Nene trusted Mrs. Houston to have a decent party with chaperones; they were neighborly and on good speaking terms. Nene knew there would be no shenanigans at that party. Renee wondered why Mrs. Houston and Nene weren't friends, perhaps it was because Nene's friends all drank cocktails in the afternoon and Mrs. Houston did not.

Dina talked about all the boys she knew who would be going to the dance and she was deciding which ones she would dance with first.

Renee didn't know if Jerry would go and if he did go, she didn't know if he would ask her to dance. She was nervous about slow dancing with boys, she had never done it before, boys didn't ask her to go to dances; they were always only friends.

She wondered if anyone would ask her to dance, she was excited yet nervous. The dance was two days away on a Saturday. She was filled with anticipation.

Renee's brothers were not going to the dance, they had a boxing rehearsal that night and they were not really interested.

Saturday rolled around and everyone was talking about the Houston dance.

Renee made sure she did all her chores, she cleaned the kitchen and bathroom, vacuumed the carpet, did the dusting and she cleaned all the little knick-knacks.

She did not want to get into trouble again. She was on punishment a long time before for neglecting her chores and "lying about Granpa." She made sure she was the perfect teenager.

Granpa was at the lodge all day. He didn't usually get home until late at night. There were never anymore nightly visits even though Aunt China wasn't there.

Aunt China was there in the afternoon for the day of the party. It was a nice summer day; there was a nice breeze. The trees were a deep green, the grass was freshly cut by her brothers, and

Nene always grew roses and tulips in the front yard. It was a storybook picture.

It was hot enough to wear a halter and mini skirt and Aunt China made sure Renee had Liz Claiborne halters and skirts.

In the evening Renee put on a green halter top with black hearts printed on it and a black miniskirt, and she had to admit she looked OK. She had big breast, a size 36 C, and she had a tiny waist, a size 26, and she had small hips, a size 34.

The colors accented her maple brown skin, her hair was a curly afro which framed her face; she had big brown eyes, thin lips and a huge white smile. She thought her worst feature was her wide nose but even that didn't look bad tonight. She looked rather good, she thought boys from out of town might like her and ask her to dance. She would love to have a boyfriend like all the other girls her age. She was seventeen and she never had a boyfriend!

It didn't look like anything would every happen with Jerry, but maybe he would come to the dance and that would change tonight. Maybe she would meet another handsome guy and finally have a boyfriend.

The party was supposed to start at 8:00 p.m. and last until 11:00 p.m. This was the first real party Renee ever went to. Everything had to be perfect. It was 8:00 p.m., but Aunt China and Nene said you should never be the first one at a party. She waited until 8:30.

Renee went next door to the party, and it looked like a different house. The furniture was taken out of the living room and dining room. There were two large tables with chips, dip, pretzels and soda and there were chairs lined up against the wall.

The lights were bright and there were streamers and "happy birthday, Reebie" signs hung all over the living room and dining room; Renee thought it looked colorful, magical, and wonderful. She was glad Nene and Aunt China reminded her it was Reebie's birthday! She got her a card and a little gift—a Jackson 5 album. She had forgotten it was Reebie's birthday. She was so excited about the dance!

There weren't many people there yet, but there were a few sitting on chairs eating snacks. The music was blasting the Isley Brothers fight the power, but no one was dancing yet. She said hello to Mrs. Houston and a few of the Houston kids who were in the kitchen, she wished Reebie a happy birthday and she gave her the birthday gift. Reebie loved the album, she was always singing and playing the piano plus she loved the Jackson 5.

They were all friendly and they told her to help herself to some snacks on the table. Renee went to get chips and dips and a soda before she had a seat along the wall. She didn't know anyone there, they must have been from out of town, it didn't look like Dorsey kids were there yet. Everyone one was in clicks talking, even the Houston kids.

Renee felt nervous and out of place, she sat down next to a girl she didn't know, and she talked to her, but she still felt nervous.

She talked about their schools and their neighborhoods; the girl was from the city; they didn't have a lot in common, but they were both excited to be there at the party.

It was nine o'clock and people started to arrive. The party got loud. Dina came in and sat next to her. Dina had on a sizzler which is a super short dress with matching short, shorts. She was smiling from ear to ear. Her outfit accentuated her curvy shape and her brown skin, her big brown eyes were sparkling with excitement and she was the star of the party. Will it go round in Circles by Billy Preston was playing loudly, they were blasting the music.

Kids were up dancing, no one was sitting down except Renee; she was bopping to the music, but no one asked her to dance. Maybe kids thought she was weird, maybe she was weird, she was kind of nervous about dancing.

Dina had not sat down since she arrived, and the Houston kids were all busy dancing. Renee thought she would probably go home without dancing with anyone when suddenly, the lights went off and there was only a dim light on, and a slow song came on. The slow song was "Make Me Say It Again Girl" by the Isley Brothers. It was Renee's favorite slow song!

She was swaying to the music when a boy from out of town asked her to dance!

CHAPTER 20
Renee's at the Houston Dance

It's the biggest dance in town. Party one day and the museum the next day.

Renee accepted and got up to dance, she didn't really know how to slow drag but she figured she would just follow what the boy did. She was nervous but she felt she did Ok, the boy asked her how she was, and he asked her name; at the end of the song, he thanked her for the dance.

He walked over to a group of people when he was finished and Renee noticed it was a few of the mean girls, they did look confident and pretty and they were probably being mean and making fun of her, but it did not ruin her night.

She had slow danced on her favorite song with a good-looking boy, and she could tell Aunt China about it, she would love it.

Around 9:30, Jerry came in, and he asked Renee to dance to "Love Train" by the O'Jays. Jerry could really dance and so could Renee when it was a fast song.

She had a real rhythm and she let loose. She even saw Dina on the dance floor, and they had a ball. They formed a soul train line, and they did crazy dances as if they were on the TV show. She was exhausted after dancing, and she went to get another glass of soda.

After that, a lot of boys asked her to dance on the fast records, but Jerry didn't ask her to dance again, he was dancing with lots of other girls at the party, they all loved him. He had on a dark blue Nehru jacket with gold trim and dark blue pants, he had a neatly cut afro and piercing brown eyes and a wide white smile. He was always very deliberate and cool, yet he had a great sense of humor, he was always the life of the party. The only girl he didn't dance with was Dina. He was always friendly to Dina, but he was friendlier with Renee, he was always at ease around Renee.

The party was about to end, and another slow song came on, it was Touch Me in The Morning by Diana Ross, Renee also loved that song and Jerry came to her chair to ask her to dance!

They dance and he talked to her and laughed with her and it was magical, Renee was floating on air and then the party was over. Jerry said he would see her at the marching practices at the lodge and in school next year. He walked Renee home after the party, but they were still only friends. Jerry didn't try to kiss her, she guessed they would only be friends, but she did love having him as a friend; He never teased her or treated her differently.

He told her he had to get home they didn't even have time to talk but he said he would talk to her at practice.

The night had ended, and Aunt China had already left, and Nene was in bed and Granpa was not home yet.

Renee went upstairs and Nene asked how the party was? Renee told her she danced and talked to her friends and she had a great time. She couldn't wait to tell Aunt China about it.

Nene was happy she had a great time, when Renee told her about the songs, they played at the dance, Nene told her about songs from her day they use to play and how she use to dance with all the boys. Some of the songs she still had on records downstairs. Maybe she would show her some of her moves one day, they both laughed.

Renee was glad the Granpa incident was behind them, she felt comfortable when she went to bed. She went to sleep and dreamed about the dance. It was a good night.

The dance was great last night, and Renee knew it would be a great day tomorrow, they were going to the museum with the church.

It was another beautiful summer day; it was a Sunday, and the church was sponsoring a trip after service.

They were going to a museum, her friend Molly from grade school was a member of the church; she was going too. She and Molly were friends from Junior high and they were still friendly in school, she and Molly could sit together on the bus.

Her brothers also went with the church on the trip to the museum in the city. It was a great day for a bus ride and museum tour.

It was sunny and warm, all the church kids and chaperones were in their Sunday best, ladies and girls wore sleeveless sundresses and men and boys wore slacks and short sleeved shirts. It was a church trip, no one wore sneakers or sports shoes, but they did wear comfortable loafers, flats and buster brown hush puppies.

Everyone piled on the bus in an orderly fashion. There were two buses, which had forty seats per bus. Everyone stood in line and waited until it was their turn to get onto the bus. Children and chaperones were lined up in two's. Each had a bus seat partner, and each waited until they were summoned to step up on the bus.

The chaperones sat in twos at the front of the bus. There were five chaperones per bus; two on each side of the bus and one right behind the bus driver. After the chaperones boarded, the children were allowed on the bus in an orderly fashion, they were checked off a list of names and walked up the bus steps and onto the vehicle.

The first groups of two went toward the back and found seats, Renee's brothers were next, they sat in the middle of the bus, Reggie Jr was the oldest and he got to sit by the window; Little Roy didn't mind, he got to talk to all his friends from the aisle.

Renee and Molly sat behind Reggie Jr and Little Roy, Renee sat by the window, Molly didn't care where she sat; she was thrilled to be on the bus on the way to a museum in the city.

Finally, everybody was on board and the buses were lined up behind one another, they waited in anticipation and they talked about how they were about to leave.

It was 12:00 p.m., and they would get to the museum at 1:00 p.m. It would be a straight bus ride to the city. There wouldn't be change overs to subways or other buses like they experienced for the ride to the concert.

They were getting hungry but luckily women in the church had packed sandwiches and soda and they all had eaten on the bus. They had a bag for garbage, and they kept the bus clean and clutter free.

The bus followed the other bus; they stayed together for the entire trip. They went through the residential neighborhoods and the kids pointed at the beautiful houses and manicured lawns. They even saw lakes and creeks and talked about going for a swim.

They passed industrial sites and wondered what was inside the big steel buildings. They sang songs and played games such as how many license plates could you count from other states. It was a great bus ride full of excited kids.

Finally, they arrived at the museum in the city. It was the Benjamin Franklin Museum. There was a large statue of Benjamin Franklin in the front of the building. Renee had of course heard of Benjamin Franklin, but she didn't really connect him to Pennsylvania.

She knew he was a Governor and he discovered electricity with a kite but that was the extent of it.

As they deboarded the bus they stood around the statue of Franklin and a tour guide from the museum provided a narration of the life of Benjamin Franklin. She talked about his discovery of electricity which Renee knew, she talked about his writings which Renee knew.

She then she talked about how he was an abolitionist and fought for the education of blacks and integration into American society. She did not remember learning about that in school.

They followed the tour guide into the Museum, it was a huge, impressive place.

There were wax figure scenes of Colonial men in clothes from the 1700s, the men wore waistcoats and stockings with pants which did not pass their knees and the women wore wide gowns.

It looked like everyone was wearing a white curly wig, women and men. Renee didn't realize they all wore wigs, she wondered if everyday people wore white wigs; she was sure slaves did not wear wigs.

The furniture was dark wood, sturdy and simple, all the wood for all the rooms seemed to match, the tables and chairs were dark wood, the bedframes were dark wood, even the floors were dark wood.

Renee loved the clothes and furnishings from the 1700s, she imagined herself back in those days but then she wondered if she would have worn the fancy gowns or if she would have been a slave. People in her family said her great, great, grandmother and great, great grandfather were slaves who moved to Virginia; they even said they worked in the white house Under President Polk in the 1840s.

It was family knowledge, Nene's Grandmother was a slave, her Mother Robin told her about her grandmother who was a slave; the family did not talk much about it. The family did talk about them being freed and buying land in Delaware and Maryland.

As a matter of fact, they still visited Uncle Randy and Aunt Laney's house which was built in Maryland in the town of Princess Mary.

Renee loved the clothes and furnishings, but she thought if she lived in that day and time, she would not be wearing the fancy gowns and she would not be sitting on sturdy, well-made furniture. She probably would have been in a cabin and working in the kitchen or maybe even in the fields.

They followed the tour guide to a letter Benjamin Franklin had written and this immediately caught Renee's attention, she loved writing and reading. They were pointing to an almanac and right next to it was a newspaper.

It seems Franklin wrote a book called Poor Richards Almanac and a newspaper called the Pennsylvania chronicle. She didn't really learn anything about Benjamin Franklin in school, she didn't know he started a college, and he was the first postmaster in Pennsylvania. What really fascinated her was his life in England and Boston before he even got to Pennsylvania. There were scenes of him signing the Declaration of Independence with a group of men, she knew one man was John Adams, but she didn't know who the rest were.

She never knew he owned slaves; it wasn't taught in school. She was glad he had a change of heart about owning slaves, Benjamin Franklin may have owned slaves, but he saw his error and became an abolitionist.

This trip to the museum was not only an interesting diversion, but it was also informative and thought provoking. They were there until 4:00 p.m., which was three hours. She couldn't believe how fast the time went; it was time to get back on the bus.

Everyone went outside and lined up by the bus and the lady checked off all the names to be sure everyone returned. It was time to go back to Dorsey to the church for the drop off.

It was 5:00 p.m. when everyone was dropped off at the church and started the walk home. It was still light out, it didn't get dark until around 8:00 p.m., and everyone walked in a crowd. They were all talking about museum exhibits, boys were talking about patriots who escaped from England and fought wars and girls were talking about mansions, crystal and China and beautiful ball gowns. Renee wondered why no one talked about there not being any black people in the nice houses with ball gowns and why did the Native Americans look poor?

These facts didn't seem to bother anyone else, but they certainly bothered Renee.

They finally reached home, and they told Nene about the museum and Renee mentioned how there were no blacks in the big houses with the fine clothes. Nene agreed, she said history has a way of glossing over facts, but she did say Benjamin Franklin had great inventions like electricity, bifocals, and printing machines. She said there was good history, but it tends to overlook inventions of other races and the atrocities of the white race.

Nene was very outspoken about race relations, yet she had friends of all races and nationalities, they didn't seem to mind her outspoken views. She spoke intelligently and she was exceptionally good at business and leadership, she was well liked and treated with respect except with Granpa.

Renee went to bed and dreamed about dances and museums and the fourth of July fireworks show that would happen next month.

When Renee woke up the next Monday morning it was a normal day. Granpa was at work, Nene was making breakfast and preparing to make dinners for restaurants in town and the boys were about to come downstairs.

Everybody ate, Renee cleaned up, the boys cut the shrubberies and grass, and Nene started to prepare her catering menu for the restaurants; she never drank until the afternoon.

Summer days were much alike. The only difference was there was no school, no studying, no homework.

The next holiday would be the Fourth of July, the marching corps practiced three times per week during the summer before the fourth of July, the band practiced and the dancers, majorettes and flag carriers practiced. Jerry was still in the band and still a great friend, but it didn't look like he would ever be romantic with Renee.

There was no other boy in the band that got Renee's attention; none were as cool, good looking or nice as Jerry. She wished they could be more than friends.

Fourth of July came, and the drum and bugle marching corps marched through the town of Dorsey, they represented the Lodge and the town people loved it, they lined the streets and waved flags and cheered on the marchers and drum and bugle corps.

Renee loved the community cheers; it was the one time of year when it seemed like the entire town came together to cheer on the parade.

It didn't seem to matter that most of the marchers in the parade were people of color, the baton twirlers, music players and dancers were so good everyone loved them, it didn't really matter what color they were.

Renee wished it could be like that every day, why were people only nice to people of different colors on holidays when they marched in parades and provided entertainment. Was it because some soldiers marched too? Were they more respectful of the military even if they were people of color? Renee only knew she loved the parades and the fourth of July shows and fireworks, the town was a nice place to live on the fourth of July.

The one good thing about the Lodge were the dances for the youth on Memorial Day, Fourth of July and other holidays. The whole town would come out and Renee wasn't as shy at those dances, then again, it wasn't the entire town; there were only black people at the town lodge dances.

She knew all the people from the marching band and drum and bugle corps, and she didn't feel self-conscious dancing. She still was a little hesitant about slow dancing, but no one asked her to slow dance at those functions. Most of the kids didn't slow dance, they were all friends and they only danced on the fast tunes, the slow tunes were for couples and there were only a few couples.

The best dance was the bump, it didn't matter if you did it with a girl or a guy, everyone was on the floor doing the bump. You would bump your hips with your partner in time with the music.

You could twirl around and bump, you could slide down to the floor and slide up and bump, it was an energetic, fun dance, it was more fun than standing in one place and bopping to the music.

The Lodge Hall dances were fun, they weren't romantic like the Houston Dance when she slow danced with a boy, but they were a fun diversion for a Saturday evening. Nene and Aunt China encouraged her to go to the dances and events. She was always tired after the lodge dances, it was always fast paced dancing and the whole crowd was always on the dance floor, you barely got to sit down; it was almost like exercise.

She liked those days in the summer. The marching band and her friends Fawn and Dina always gave her something to do, but the summer was coming to an end.

The hot summer days and evenings with green trees, roses and tulips were turning into cooler days and nights. The tree leaves were starting to turn yellow, and orange and it was the beginning of September. Renee would be going back to school; this would be her senior year.

She wondered about her friends in school and the new subjects she would learn. This year she would take harder subjects, such as different languages and harder math such as calculus and trigonometry.

Renee was in College Prep courses; she would also need to think about which college she was going to attend.

CHAPTER 21
High School Prom Plans?

Aunt China came over one evening and reminded her about going to her Prom, she said her prom was magical. She reminisced about her prom in a fancy hotel with wonderful decorations and music.

She went with her boyfriend Freddy and they danced the night away, she didn't get home until 1:00 a.m. in the morning, Aunt China said she would never forget it.

She wore a gold satin gown with a bow in the back and gold gloves which came to her elbows. She said Renee could not miss her prom, it would be one of her fondest memories. Aunt China asked if any boy asked her to the prom and Renee told her no one asked her. She reminded her; you must let boys know you were interested in going to the prom.

Renee was mortified, she didn't think anyone would say yes but of course she thought of Jerry first. She was afraid Jerry would say no because he always hung out with girls from out of town. She would see who else was in school for her Senior Year. Maybe there would be someone else.

Reggie Junior would be in tenth grade and Little Roy would be in ninth grade, they would both be in high school with her. She wondered if she would see them in school, but they had different lunch periods and their classes probably would not be near each other.

It would still be nice to have her brothers in the same school, she remembered walking to school with them in elementary school and junior high. It would be nice to walk home from school with them, it wasn't that far away; it was just down the block.

It was finally the first day of school Renee and her brothers had gotten new outfits and notebooks and pencils. The day was warm for September; it was 85 degrees.

The trees had started to turn but it was a warm day. Renee wore a short sleeve shirt and bell-bottom pants; her hair was in an afro and she had big hoop earrings. She thought she looked surprisingly good. She was 5'7 inches and 110 pounds. She was still tall and thin with a big chest. She had big brown eyes, long eyelashes, a flat nose, and thin lips.

She didn't like her nose. She thought it was too big, but she thought she looked nice. Her brothers wore short sleeve shirts and slacks, they had small afros; they were also thin with big eyes.

They walked down the street to the high school and the cool kids were outside smoking.

They nodded hello and Renee introduced them to her brothers before they went inside, they had to separate because their classes were in different parts of the building.

Before they separated Renee went to the office with them to get their schedules. Once they got their schedules, they separated to find their classes, she went to her first class which was history, a subject she really liked.

The history teacher was a tall thin man who talked about patriots and George Washington, she wondered why history class had only one chapter which covered accomplishments of people of color.

She still loved history, she liked to imagine what it was like living in the 1700s and 1800s she just wanted to know more about the black people in those times.

She liked her next class better; it was Spanish, and second languages came easy to Renee. The teacher would play a Spanish record and the class would repeat the record, they would then have to repeat it to other people in the class.

They would ask a classmate a simple question in Spanish and the classmate would answer in Spanish. The teacher always corrected their accent and Renee became comfortable with it. She thought she was going to be particularly good with Spanish.

Some of the students had a difficult time speaking, it seemed like the boys had an especially hard time. She didn't know if it was shyness or inability.

Spanish class went quickly, and it was time for English, Renee always liked English and was looking forward to the class.

English was one of her favorite classes, she didn't mind English homework because it allowed her to read good novels; she didn't even mind writing the summary paper assignments. She loved reading but she wasn't fond of some of the authors the teachers wanted her to write about.

Sometimes the teacher would allow them to choose their own book and she would sometimes make up books and write a book report on the book she made up. She would complete a bibliography using her name and she got A's on the papers. She would do the paper on the subject the teacher suggested, and she would follow the rules the teachers requested but she would make up the book. When she told Aunt China and Nene what she did and showed them the good grade they didn't yell, if the teacher gave her A's, it must have been ok.

She only did this a couple of times, normally teachers usually assigned fascinating books such as Shakespeare, Edgar Allan Poe, Alice Walker, Maya Angelo, Richard Wright, Langston Hughes or Nikki Giovanni. She always waited until the last minute to write the papers, but she loved reading the books.

Renee looked around at the students in her class, most of them were the same students from Junior High, she was friends with a couple of them, even the mean girls treated her with grudging respect.

The black boys were the same boys she knew from school, she was friendly with them, but she was never romantically involved with any of them, she liked them, but they only saw her as a friend.

The white boys were ok but there were no interracial couples in her school.

It didn't look like she would have a boyfriend from school this year, she couldn't imagine talking to them about the prom. Jerry wasn't in any of her classes, she would have to wait until drum and bugle practice to see him, maybe he would say yes to the prom.

He also joined the marching band for the school, he was the drum major for the high school marching band, he carried a big stick which was called a drum major's mace. The crowd went wild at games when the marching band was on the field, Jerry was always popular with everyone in the school.

For now, Renee was still in English class and the teacher gave them an assignment before they left, they were supposed to read a book by a new Author, Stephen King.

Renee heard of his novel Carrie, but she didn't read the book. She even heard rumors of a movie coming out about the novel Carrie.

The teacher told them to read Kings book Salem's Lot, and to write a paper about it, Renee was disappointed, she had hoped the assignment would be Carrie. Most of the class was excited about reading Stephen King, he was a good writer who wrote scary stories. She was excited to read a new Author, especially one who wrote scary stories; this is probably why she loved Edgar Allan Poe.

She headed to the school library to get the book after classes and much to her delight the library wasn't crowded, she guessed the other students hadn't gotten there yet. She checked out a copy of Salem's Lot and decided she would start reading it after school, the teacher gave them a month to read it, it would count toward their midterm grade.

It was time to walk home from school and Renee saw her Brothers in the school yard, they were getting ready to walk home. She also saw Jerry, Dina and Molly. They all started walking and talking about their school day, Jerry talked about his classes, but he was most excited about the band and the music and marching practices.

Dina wasn't excited about any of the school subjects, she was excited about a new boy she met, she sure was lucky; boys always noticed her, he would probably be her boyfriend and ask her to the prom before the week was finished.

Her brothers were excited about wood shop, they would be making things like ashtrays and jewelry boxes and other things made of wood. Little Roy was excited about making things, but Reggie Jr was more excited about a business and science classes he was taking. He said the business class would follow the stock market, and the science class would take field trips in town and to the creek.

Renee remembered the business class, she got a B in it, but it didn't really excite her, she didn't follow the stock market except for homework.

She told them about the Stephen King book she was going to read, they all heard about his writing; everybody knew how scary he was. Jerry read Carrie and he said it was one of the scariest books he ever read, he was reading "Salem's Lot" now and he said it was even scarier than Carrie. He said they were long books but so good he read them quickly. Renee could not wait to start the book, Jerry had good taste in books; he had good taste in everything.

Nene asked Renee and her Brothers about the first day of school, her brothers told her about wood shop and Renee told her about her Stephen King book. Nene told Reggie Jr and Little Roy about Grandpa building things and wood shop being a plus, boys should always know how to build things.

She told Renee how she heard Stephen King was a good writer and she figured Renee would get a kick out of him. She told her to read the book and get the paper out of the way, don't procrastinate,

Renee wondered if she got her desire for reading from Nene, Nene loved to read, she had novels about slavery and romance and wars on bookshelves all over the house.

The kids were always told they were not allowed to read those books, they were for adults only, so of course they snuck and read them; Nene probably told them not to read them to pique their interest.

Renee usually snuck and read the novels about slavery, they were always stories about mansions and fine white ladies and rich slave masters. Sometimes the rich masters would have affairs with the slave women, sometimes the slave would get pregnant and have a half black child; in extreme circumstances they would kill the child. In some circumstances the slave master's wife would punish the slave, but she would keep the slave around.

Sometimes, the slave master's wife would sleep with the male slave and of course the male slave would be punished for rape. The books were fascinating, and Nene never said anything if she found one missing. She wanted the kids to read, she always said reading will always help with your education and a good education will even the playing field.

Everyone started their homework, it took Renee about an hour to complete her Spanish, Math, History and Science homework. She could now start to read her Stephen King Book so she could get her book report done early in the school year. She was quite excited.

The school year continued, and Renee read the Stephen King book "Salem's Lot" for her English class and she decided he was one of her new favorite authors. His books were scary, believable and addicting, she was an absolute fan; she even considered starting a fan club. She had plenty of time to complete her book report for English class, she would start on it in a few weeks.

It was October and time for Halloween, Renee was much too old for Trick or treating and she didn't like Halloween parties; she would be eighteen this year and her brothers were fifteen and sixteen. They were all too old for trick or treating and they didn't usually like Halloween parties, but the school was having a party which sounded like fun.

They were going to have pizza and soda and candy and students were going to dress up like their favorite people.

CHAPTER 22
There's a Halloween Party

Who will win the costume contest?

Renee was going to dress up like Chaka Khan, her brothers were going to dress up like shaft from the movies and JJ from the show Good Times. This sounded like it could be a lot of fun, it was going to be next Friday night after school.

Renee called Aunt China in the evening after school to tell her about the Halloween party next week, she told her she wanted to dress like Chaka Khan. Aunt China told her she would be over Sunday to get her outfit ready.

When she came over that Sunday, she had a long Afro wig and she fixed it, so it framed Renee's face and it hung down her back, Renee loved it! She also picked out a black skirt mini skirt, black boots, and a black vest, she would put a white T shirt under the vest; Aunt China drew big red lips on it just like Chaka Khan. Renee was ready, she couldn't wait for the party.

Reggie Jr had bell bottoms, a paint easel, a beret and a shirt with Dyno mite written on it for his JJ costume. Little Roy had a black leather jacket with leather bell bottoms and black leather gloves, Aunt China made him a mustache and he would get a shape up and look just like shaft.

They couldn't wait, they were sure they would look great, maybe they would even win the costume prize, it was $25 for third prize, $50 for second prize, and $100 for first prize! Renee thought they would give everyone stiff competition in the costume category. It was five days away!

It was finally the day of the Halloween party, school that day seemed to last forever; Renee liked all her classes, but she couldn't wait to get home to do her homework, eat dinner and get ready for the party.

The whole school was buzzing about the party, but Dina was being very secretive about her costume, she said she would not tell anybody about it until the party. No one was saying anything about their costumes, everyone would have to wait for the party for the big reveal. They all walked home together talking excitedly about the upcoming festivities, but everyone kept their secrets about the costumes.

Renee rushed through her homework, she still did not start her book report, she read the book and it wasn't due until next month; she had plenty of time. She did her math, chemistry, history and vocabulary words for English; she was done her homework. Her brothers were in their room doing their homework, it was five o'clock when they finished, and it was time to go down to dinner.

Nene made them eat a light dinner even though there was going to be pizza at the party, she said pizza is not dinner. They gulped down fried fish, green beans and mashed potatoes; they wanted to hurry and get into their costumes.

Renee put on the black skirt, white T shirt with the lips and the black vest and it fit every curve although the most curve she had was her big chest. She had a tiny waist and long thin legs; she wore black boots to match her outfit. This outfit really complimented her figure! She heard Aunt China downstairs and she was glad; she would make sure the wig and make up was perfect. Aunt China came upstairs just as Renee was putting on the afro wig, it framed her face, her big brown eyes were bright, and she felt gorgeous. Aunt China loved it, but she added red lipstick like Chaka Khan, she followed it with eyelashes and eye shadow. Renee was sure everybody would know who she was, and she was positive she would win the contest.

She went downstairs to show Nene and Nene thought the skirt was too short and the make-up was too much, but Aunt China told her the point was to look like Chaka Khan and have a chance at the $100 prize.

Nene agreed with Aunt China about that, she never went against a chance to make money if it was legal. Aunt China went upstairs to help Reggie Jr and Little Roy.

The boys finally came downstairs, and Nene loved their costumes Little Reggie who was "JJ" had on a black beret and carried a paint color palette and paint brush. He had "Dy-No-Mite" drawn on his shirt.

Little Roy had on black leather from head to toe, he was wearing a leather jacket, pants, shoes and even leather gloves; he was also wearing a mustache. They were all ready to go to the party.

They wondered if people would know who they were before they told them, they thought so; they couldn't imagine anyone who didn't know who they were dressed up to be. They started to dream about what they would do with their winnings; they were sure these were the best costumes.

They walked up to the school and saw a few people walking ahead of them, they didn't know who they were, these students must be from different parts of town. Renee and her brothers were still not worried, they didn't think the costumes of the other students were that great.

There was a rock star, Renee couldn't tell who it was supposed to be, and a movie star? Renee and her brothers couldn't tell who they were supposed to be. Reggie Jr. and Little Roy remarked. The three of them might win the top three prizes.

They walked into the gym which had been decorated for Halloween. There were skeletons, witches, ghost and streamers hanging around the entire gym, and of course there were Happy Halloween signs. They couldn't believe how the gym had been transformed.

She started to look around at the costumes, there were rock stars and movie stars, but Renee couldn't tell who they were supposed to be. It looked like their only competition might be a boy dressed like Paul McCartney and a girl dressed like Cher.

Reggie Jr. was really hamming it up, with his shouts of Dy-No-Mite and his huge smile, the crowd loved it! He was good, he might want to think about acting for a career goal. Renee walked around singing tell me something good and everyone seemed to like it. Little Roy walked around singing shaft, but Renee and little Roy was sure Reggie Jr and his Dy-No-Mite exclamations would win first prize.

Everyone was eating pizza, dancing, and looking at costumes right before the costume prizes were going to be announced, when suddenly a hush fell over the room. In walked Dina, she had a long curly wig which hung down her back, and a long sequin gown. She had a boa wrapped loosely around her neck and long dangling earrings. She started saying hello everyone, she stretched out her hands and started singing reach out and touch somebody's hand.

Dina was the belle of the ball, even Renee had to admit she had the best costume of the night. Everyone in the room knew who won first prize.

She was fabulous. She walked over to Renee and said, "What do you think?" Renee said, "Girl, you won." The only question now was who won second and third prize.

It was finally time to judge the costumes and all the participating students lined up to be judged. They all had a name and number attached to their costume, each person in the audience was given a piece of paper to cast their vote for the name and number of their choice.

There were three teachers who counted the votes and passed the results to the judges. The judges had each contestant step up under the light so they could show off the costumes, the crowd clapped for all the costumes, but they seemed to like the Paul McCartney and Mick Jagger costumes the best so far.

It was time for Little Roy to go under the spotlight as shaft, the crowd liked him, and he got a hearty applause, but she couldn't tell if it was more applause than the Mick Jagger costume. It was a good thing they had paper ballots because it was hard to tell by applause.

Reggie Jr. went up next as JJ and the applause was thunderous. They really liked the JJ costume and Reggie Jr.'s antics. She started to wonder if he could get first prize.

It was time for Renee to go up and she strutted up to the stage with her miniskirt, boots, and long afro. There was more thunderous applause; she didn't know she was so popular. It sounded like her and Reggie Jr got the same applause, she couldn't figure if one of them won or both won.

Finally, finally Dina glided on the stage with her boa and sequin gown, she tossed her curly afro which came down to the small of her back, she blew kisses at the crowd and started singing reach out and touch. The crowd was on their feet cheering, it was obvious who would win first place; Renee and her brothers were clapping along with the crowd. Maybe they would win second or third prize.

The contest was finished, and it was time to announce the votes. Third prize went to Mick Jagger, he did a little dance and started singing "I can't get no satisfaction" the crowd loved it.

The second prize was Reggie Jr.! He won, and he would get $50! Regina and Dina were jumping and shouting. Reggie Jr came on stage strutting and shouting Dyno mite! He smiled from ear to ear as he collected his trophy and a $50 check, he gave the judges a soul brother handshake and the crowd was screaming and whistling. Renee was sure Dina won first prize, no other costume came close to hers; Dina said it would be nice, but she wasn't sure, she said Renee's costume was great too, she wouldn't be surprised if Renee won.

First prize was finally called, and it was Dina, she glided up to the stage and got her first prize trophy and check for $100. She was smiling from ear to ear and tossing her hair, she was thrilled but she was upset that Renee didn't get a prize, she thought Renee's outfit was better than Mick Jaggers.

Renee was glad two people in her group got prizes although she would have loved to walk out with a check and a trophy. They walked home and Dina told Renee she would treat her to some nail polish at Woolworth's next week after she cashed her check.

Renee and her brothers went home. It was 9:00 p.m., and Aunt China was still there. They told her and Nene how Reggie Jr. won second price and got a trophy and $50. He showed them his JJ impression and they all laughed and congratulated him.

Nene told him he should deposit his check in his savings account and Little Reggie said he had already placed the check inside his savings account passbook. They went to their rooms and watched TV and Renee listened to records before they fell asleep.

It was November and Regina realized she had not done her book report on Stephen King, it was due Monday and today was Saturday; Nene was right, she shouldn't have procrastinated. She would eat breakfast, do her chores and do her book report, no matter how long it took; she didn't like to take more than a day to do a book report. It had to be three pages so it would probably take her a couple of hours.

She finished her chores and started on the book report, she remembered it because she liked it, but she had the book beside her just in case she forgot something.

She followed the printout the teachers gave them and started with his name, hometown and the date the book was written. She refreshed her memory on Bibliographies, and she started answering the questions and writing the report.

She found it easy but there was so much to write, Renee thought it might take longer than three hours and she was already getting tired. It was only the middle of the afternoon, but book reports seemed to take forever. The questions asked about things which happened throughout the book and Renee didn't even need to look it up. She remembered everything about *Salem's Lot*. She remembered the scary people; the vampires were terrifying; she was afraid the entire town was going to be taken over and she wondered if good would really overtake evil.

She compared it to the good and evil struggle of life, good might overtake evil but it might take a while. In some instances, it might seem like good doesn't overcome evil. She wrote for hours even though she would have preferred to listen to records or watch TV. She finally finished the report and she thought it was good, she figured she'd get a B which was fine with her.

Renee got her grade back the next week and she got an A, the teacher told her she should consider writing. Renee told her she wrote for the school newspaper and the teacher said she should consider writing in college and for a career.

She knew she would go to college, but she always thought she would major in sociology or psychology, she wanted a field where she could help people. She thought her calling was managing groups and group therapy for different people. She always thought it was a good idea for people with similar problems to talk about it in the open and heal from it.

A few colleges had good sociology programs and she would apply to them, maybe she would also apply to a journalist program. She thanked the teacher for the writing suggestions, but she didn't know if she would like writing for the rest of her life, then again; writing for a newspaper didn't sound so bad.

It was time to get ready for Christmas and shop for a Christmas outfit, this was always Renee's favorite time of the year.

CHAPTER 23
Christmas Shopping and Prom Dress Discussions

Where is Mom? Could Larry from the band be a prom date?

She had already bought her Christmas gifts; she and her brothers still had a Christmas savings account and they used it every year; it was $100 now. They would buy gifts and they could use the leftover money to buy a Christmas outfit.

They had bought Christmas gifts from Woolworth and Sears and they walked to a Rainbow shop in town, Renee was looking at a beautiful green dress with red trim.

Aunt China looked over at racks of dresses, which had a big sign displayed that said Prom dresses. Aunt China told her they would need to look at Prom dresses after Renee bought her Christmas outfit.

They grabbed the pretty green dress for Christmas, and they walked over to the Prom dresses. These were not dresses; these were gowns. Renee couldn't imagine wearing a beautiful gown like that. She knew she would look nice in the gowns; she was

5'7 and a size 6, she had a tiny waist, long legs and a big chest; she kept her curly afro perfectly picked, Aunt China told her she would need to get her hair straightened for evening wear. Renee agree, she would need straight hair to go with a gown.

Aunt China and Renee looked at blue, purple and green gowns made of satin, silk and lace. Finally, Renee saw a pink satin gown, it was A-line with a cinched waist; there was a bow on the back, it was dazzling.

Aunt China talked about her prom and the wonderful time she had. She talked about her yellow gown made of satin and silk and she reminisced about it being one of the greatest days in her life.

The pink gown was 49.99, she would have to get Daddy to help her buy it, she didn't have enough money.

While fantasizing about wearing the dress she realized a horrible fact, Renee did not have a date for the prom! Jerry was dating a girl from out of town, Alvin and Denny liked her, but they already had dates for the prom, she realized she might not get to go to the prom.

She didn't think any of the boys would ask her! She had friends but no boys ever asked her to be anything more than friends.

She paid for her Christmas outfit and went home depressed. Was she going to miss her high school prom?

Christmas and New Year passed, Renee and her brothers spent time with Daddy, aunts, uncles, and cousins, but Mommy never came around. They still went to Nene Boye's house and got gifts from that side of the family, but Mommy was never there either. They guessed she spent holidays with her husband and daughters.

The holidays were over, and it was time to go back to school, Renee got good grades at the end of the semester in December, and she was feeling confident. The holidays were over, and the prom was the big subject; everyone talked about who they would go with and what they would wear. They were even asking students to join the prom committee. Renee didn't want to join the committee since she figured she wouldn't be going. She figured she would graduate and go to college.

Renee told Aunt China about her problem of getting a date for the prom. Aunt China told Renee how pretty she was, she said with her shape she could be a model and she had a pretty face with big brown eyes and thin nice lips. She said she could ask any boy to go to the prom, but Renee was mortified, she didn't want to ask someone and have them turn her down and laugh at her. It didn't look like she was going to the prom.

Renee was friendly with the boys, they laughed and cut up with her, but none asked her to the prom.

When she asked them who they were going to the prom with they would tell her who they were taking, or they would say they don't know. No one asked her to go, and she was too afraid to ask.

It was February and she still did not have a date for the prom, Nene and Aunt China started to worry and they told Daddy.

Daddy introduced her to one of the band members in his singing group who was four years older than her.

His name was Larry. He played the guitar and sang lead on some songs. Daddy took her and Aunt China to one of their performances at the club where they sometimes played. Larry had a silky-smooth voice and the ladies swooned, he was tall; he must have been 6'4, he had smooth brown skin, a neat afro and a big white smile. He had deep penetrating dark eyes, a thin nose and full lips, he was gorgeous and talented.

After each set, he took Renee outside and talked to her about his dreams in the music world and his favorite books and movies. He had a deep, rich, melodic voice yet he had a country twang. She asked about the accent and he told her about his family coming from Virginia and settling in PA. Renee thought that was probably why he was so nice, polite and different from any guy she knew. She loved talking to him, he loved to talk, and he loved to hear her talk, he said she had a northern accent and they laughed. She could talk to him for hours, but he had to get back to his music sets.

After one music set, they talked about the movie Carrie and how scary it was, Larry said it even terrified him, they had similar taste in movies.

They talked about Stephen King and their favorite music groups, they both loved the same type of music and movies; the night was magical. Before Larry went back to his last musical set, he told Renee her Dad mentioned she had a prom coming up in May and he asked if he could take her! Renee was floored, she couldn't believe this gorgeous guy who could have any girl/woman in club asked her to the prom!

He asked her why she was surprised, He told her how pretty she was; and how she could be a model and he couldn't believe how smart and nice she was. He said any guy would be proud to have her on his arm. She was floating on air as she said yes, she finally had a date for the prom, and he was a guy anyone would love to go with.

He took Renee's chin in his hand and kissed her on the nose. They laughed before he went into the club to finish, he set.

Renee went to see him perform a couple of times after that, he would take her outside between breaks and they would talk about everything.

One night before his last set they were laughing and he then became serious, he told her she was the prettiest, smartest, nicest girl he had met in a long time and kissed her on the lips, it was a deep full kiss. Renee thought she would faint, she had kissed a few boys before, but it was nothing like this.

He asked for her phone number and he told her he would call her tomorrow. She went into the club to see the last set; she could not stop daydreaming and smiling.

On the ride home she told Daddy and Aunt China Larry asked her to the prom and Daddy said he was a nice guy and he approved. Aunt China said he was cute, and they would have to go get a prom dress.

Both Daddy and Aunt China said he would have to come to Renee's house for dinner and of course he would come over when they practiced with the singing group.

Daddy said Larry had been there with the singing group before, but Renee never noticed, she just figured he was one of the men in Daddy's singing group and she never really looked at them.

Renee was glad to go back to school Monday, she told all her classmates about her prom date, she talked about how he played in a band and was tall, worldly and gorgeous. She didn't think most students believed her because she never had a boyfriend, and they couldn't imagine her showing up with the person she was describing. Most of them were going with boys from school or boys from other neighborhoods, she imagined they would be shocked when she walked into the prom with Larry. She couldn't wait until after school, Larry said he would call tonight.

She went to classes and noticed signs for a job fair from 3:00 to 5:00 p.m. It was 2:00 p.m. and she noticed people setting up tables with banners for big companies. She assumed she would go to college after school. She already had acceptance letters from Penn State, Cheyney College, and a NY college, but she would check out the job fair after classes.

There were many companies at the job fair, and Renee was curious. There were a lot of Gas companies such as Exxon, Shell, Texaco, Mobil; they said they had clerical positions which paid a decent salary and benefits, but she wasn't interested. She could not imagine typing all day for an oil company.

She headed over to a table which displayed a banner of AT&T technologies, they said there would be groundbreaking innovations, but she just pictured telephone operators and she left the table. She could not imagine typing all day for a phone company or connecting phone calls at a switchboard.

She saw a bunch of food companies such as Nabisco, General Mills, Pepsi, Sara Lee but they didn't interest her either, she couldn't imagine herself typing all day for any of those companies; she even wondered if she would end up in an assembly line.

She saw tables for CBS and RCA, and they caught her attention. She went to the CBS table and there was a pretty lady with a bright smile and long blond hair and big blue eyes. She asked Renee if she got good grades and how many words per minute she typed. She typed sixty words per minute and she of course got good grades. The lady was impressed. She said she could start out in the typing pool and end up as an administrative assistant for a news show. There was no stopping her.

Renee was extremely interested; this did not sound like a dead-end job. She completed applications, took business cards and was leaving the job fair when she saw a cartoon picture with a slogan which said, "Uncle Sam wants you to join the Army."

She also saw tables with Marine slogans, one said "if everybody could get into the Marines, it wouldn't be the marines."

There were tables representing every branch of the military and Renee was intrigued. The military sounded interesting to her, she would get to travel, and she would be trained to use weapons, for some reason that thought appealed to her.

She stopped by the table with the information about the Marines, but it didn't really appeal to her, she liked the uniforms but there were no women at the table. She liked the Navy uniforms, but she couldn't imagine being on a ship every day, she was not a great swimmer and she was afraid she would feel trapped.

She liked the air force, the uniforms were great and there was a woman who told her about how she could be in an air force squadron and how exciting it would be to travel to different countries, she also talked about salary and benefits. Renee got information about the air force.

The last table she saw was the table with the "Uncle Sam wants you to join the Army" poster. She walked up to the Army Table and there was a black lady in a green. Crisp, uniform, she looked regal. There were men at the Army table, but the black lady caught Renee's attention.

She told Renee how she was stationed all over the US and in different countries, she explained how the army made sure you were in shape, they made sure you learned how to handle weapons and then you went to Army School to learn your trade or MOS. The Army sounded fascinating to Renee, she liked the idea of traveling and handling rifles.

She liked the idea of the respect people would show her if she went into the military and wore her uniform when she visited home.

She could imagine herself in the Army or Air Force and visiting home in uniform. She didn't think she would live at home after school, she wanted to get away and explore the world. She took a lot of the Army and air force information.

She didn't tell Nene or her brothers about her military information, but she did tell them about CBS and RCA. Nene said they sounded like good jobs, but she should think of getting her college degree, she said you could go further with a college degree.

Renee did her homework and looked at TV and in the middle of Good Times the phone rang, and it was Larry for her! There were two phones in the house, one was downstairs in the dining room, and one was upstairs in the hallway; Nene said she could take the call on the upstairs extension. Nene and her brothers smiled knowingly as she ran upstairs to get the phone, Granpa was looking at Good times and laughing at the show, he didn't react to the phone call.

Renee picked up the upstairs phone and Larry's smooth voice said Hi, how're you doing? What did you do today? Renee told him about the job fair and the different companies and the military. Larry said he couldn't imagine her typing all day either, he worked as a mechanic and at a warehouse all day and he practiced with the band at night. He wanted to concentrate on the music, he couldn't wait until he made enough money to quit the jobs, they had shows every weekend; he hoped he would be able to quit the other jobs soon.

He thought college and a company like RCA or CBS sounded better than the military, but he could imagine her doing anything she decided to do. He said on top of being pretty she seemed to have a steely resolve.

She told him when he's famous with the band she wanted his autograph, he said he thought he could arrange that, and they laughed. Nene had told her to invite Larry for a meal and she invited him to Saturday dinner, Larry said he would be glad to come.

She told him Nene was an excellent cook and he would really enjoy the food, people came from all over for her dinners. He said he was glad about the food but the cherry on top was getting to see her. He reminded her about coming to more of his shows, Daddy was at some of the shows, he liked Larry and encouraged it.

Renee said she would not miss it for the world, he had one of the best voices she had ever heard, and she was used to good singing voices; her Dad and Aunt China and people who came to their house had great singing voices. Larry reminded her he practiced at her house before, it was strange he never noticed her; she must have been out.

Renee was floating on air as she went to school, people were starting to believe she really did have a great date for the prom. She was more outgoing and confident; she told her classmates about going to clubs to see him perform and having him over for dinner.

Saturday came and Larry was coming to dinner, Nene asked him what his favorite foods were, and she cooked all of them. Dinner was 6:00 p.m. and he came early at 4:00 p.m. Aunt China came over also. They listened to music, sang and danced, everyone in the family loved Larry, even her brothers. After singing and dancing they watched TV, they were laughing at George Jefferson when Nene announced dinner being ready.

They usually ate at the kitchen table, but dinner tonight was at the dining room table.

The table was set with China and crystal-like Thanksgiving and the food was like Christmas. There was Baked ham, which was baked and sizzling with glaze and cloves, there were golden brown Cornish hens, there were collard greens with ham hocks, there were green beans with neck bones, there was potato salad and macaroni and cheese which was dripping with cheese, it looked like the cheese stuck to every bit of macaroni. Nene really did cook all of Larry's favorites.

Everyone sat down to dinner and oohed and aahed at the beautiful spread and to top it off Nene brought out homemade biscuits. Everyone in the family dug in except for Granpa, he was not at home, he was at the lodge.

They didn't have Cornish game hens every day and Renee, Aunt China and her brothers dug in, Larry dug into the ham, he had two helpings of everything, and Nene loved it.

He said it was the best meal he had ever had, he asked Nene why she wasn't eating, and she answered she'd been tasting all day and she wasn't ready to eat yet. After dinner they were stuffed, they were sure they could not eat another bite until Nene brought out the home-made apple pie.

They could not pass up homemade apple pie, Larry sure could eat, it was amazing he could stay so thin if he always ate like that, but then again, Renee ate a lot too and she was tall and thin. She guessed they had a fast metabolism, her brothers and Aunt China and her Dad were tall and thin, and they all had big appetites,

Granpa was also tall and thin, it must have run in the family. Nene was short and thin, she looked like her father, she even had the same build as him.

Renee would normally have to do the dishes but Aunt China and Nene did them so she could sit in the living room and watch TV with Larry after dinner. Her brothers had gone upstairs, and Nene and Aunt China were in the kitchen cleaning up. This gave Renee and Larry a chance to sit close and cuddle and watch TV, they even stole a couple of kisses.

It was 8:00 p.m., and Larry suggested they take a walk around Dorsey; she could show him the sights.

CHAPTER 24
Larry Is a Big Hit with Renee, the Family, and the Town

She said there weren't many sites, but she would show him a few of her favorite places. She asked Nene if she minded if her and Larry took a walk and Nene said sure, but they had to be back by 10:00 p.m. Aunt China said Nene should give them until 11:00 p.m., there was a dance at the lodge, and they wouldn't want to come back right after they got there. Nene agreed but she said they had better be back by 11:00 p.m. on the dot, not a minute later.

Larry didn't seem to mind an 11:00 p.m. curfew, he thought it was quite reasonable and he agreed to make sure they were back by no later than 11:00 p.m.

Nene and Aunt China loved his manners and his good looks, they were quite impressed with Larry, he was four years older than Renee, but that was okay. She was eighteen; he had just turned twenty-two. Daddy wasn't there he would come to Sunday dinner tomorrow, but he also loved Larry's personality and manners. Larry was practically part of the family. Renee was thrilled.

They walked the streets of Dorsey holding hands and Renee showed him her favorite spots. The streetlights were on and it was well lit. It was a brisk March night, and they wore jackets, the air was electric and exhilarating. Renee was surprised he didn't take his car, but he said he wanted to walk and show her off.

They walked to the corner store to get gum and soda still holding hands and they ran into people from the neighborhood and from school. Renee introduced Larry as her friend from Philly. They continued walking to the high school and Larry pushed her on the swings. There was no one on the high school grounds and Larry kissed her under the tree, he caressed her shoulders and back, and Renee felt like she was on fire. She had kissed a few boys but none of them made her feel like this, she didn't want to stop kissing him. They continued to walk holding hands, shoulder to shoulder and they walked toward the lodge dance.

The Lodge was brightly lit, you could see the lights and hear the loud music before you approached it. There were classmates and teens from town hanging outside, Renee introduced them all to Larry. He was comfortable with everybody; he was always brimming with confidence.

They walked into the lodge and the dance was already in full session, students were dancing to "Play That Funky Music." Renee introduced people in the club to Larry and she walked over to Dina.

Dina was all smiles, she had on a "Sizzler" which is a short dress and matching shorts and she looked perfect with a curly afro and make-up. Renee was a little worried, what if Larry liked Dina more than her? Renee thought she looked rather good herself, she had on a mini skirt, a blouse and boots, she also had a curly afro and Aunt China helped with her make up. She thought Dina's curvy shape was better than hers, but Renee thought she was no slouch herself; she was tall with big boobs and long thin legs that went up to her thighs; Dina was shorter with curvy legs and big boobs.

Renee introduced Larry to Dina, and he was his joking and charming. He told her they would see her later and Larry pulled Renee on the floor to dance. She couldn't believe he left Dina there, but another boy asked her to dance right away. They were all on the dance floor twirling and dipping to "A Fifth of Beethoven." The night was magical.

"Love Hangover" by Diana Ross came on and everybody formed a Soul Train Line, they all stepped, bopped and twirled down the middle of the line for the entire song, they even kept it going during "Boogie Fever" by the Sylvers. The night and the dance were intoxicating.

Larry went to the bathroom and Renee talked to Dina. Dina told Renee how lucky she was, she said Larry was gorgeous and nice and boy could he dance.

Renee told her she was going to the prom with him, and Dina said she was so lucky; she would be going with Denny one of their classmates.

Denny was good looking and funny, he had a job at the gas station, and he had a souped-up car; he had an OK personality, but Renee thought Larry was better looking and taller. She also thought Larry had a nicer personality and he danced better.

She asked Dinah why Denny was not at the dance and she said he had to work. She also asked her if she bought her gown yet and she said no, Renee suggested they go together with her Aunt China, since Dina's Mom couldn't take her.

Dina's mother worked during the week and she was usually gone on the weekends. Dina thought shopping with Renee and her Aunt China was a great idea, she loved hanging with them.

She could use the money she won at the Halloween party; she saved $75 of it; she should be able to get a nice gown.

The girls were talking about prom gowns and graduation when Larry came back, he asked what the intense conversation was about, and they replied prom gowns. Larry told her to let him know about the color of her gown, he wanted to be sure they were matching on prom night. He could get a matching shirt, bow tie or cummerbund.

They asked what a cummerbund was, and he explained it's a wide sash that ties around the waist and goes under a tux; it usually matches a bow tie. They sometimes wore them with tuxes at shows.

The dance was coming to an end, Renee and Larry danced the last dance, the song was "Sweet Thing" by Rufus featuring Chaka Khan; it was one of her favorite slow songs.

Larry held her tightly as they moved slowly to the music, he even whirled her around the floor once or twice. Unlike the other party, she had no problem slow dancing, Larry was amazingly easy to follow, the fit together like a glove. He exuded so much confidence she became confident, and people stopped to look at them on the dance floor.

She felt like a different person, she felt like she was popular and part of the crowd; they were quite a hit that night. It felt like a new beginning.

Larry walked Renee home, they passed corner stores and neat manicured houses with maple trees on the sidewalks as they walked home. Finally, they arrived, and Larry kissed Renee good night and got in his car to drive home, he blew her a kiss and took off for Phila.

She walked into the house at 10:30 p.m. and Nene and Aunt China asked her how the dance was? She told them about the music and soul train line, she demonstrated how everybody was dancing, and she told them what a good dance Larry was.

Aunt China Renee and her brothers turned on the record player and danced a soul train line in the living room, they were laughing and dancing; Nene laughed but she said they had to stop.

She explained it was getting late and the music was loud, they didn't want to wake up the entire neighborhood.

Aunt China got ready to leave to go home but she told Renee they needed to go gown shopping for the prom next Saturday. She took a personal day so they could go early in the morning and take all day if they need to.

Renee asked where they were going to get the money for a gown and Nene said Daddy had given her money. She asked if Dina could go along, she explained how she had her own money from the Halloween contest for a gown and Aunt China said of course.

Next Saturday was going to be fantastic; she couldn't wait to tell Dina.

Monday in school Renee told Dina about going gown shopping Saturday, they were excitedly talking about which stores to go to. Would they go in town to a local shop, or would they go to Phila? They would wait and see, for now it was classes and homework plus Renee was going to complete the Army application, she wanted to keep her options open.

Renee was doing homework after school on Thursday, and she got a call from an Army recruiter, they wanted her to come to the recruitment station to discuss joining the Army. They explained the exotic places she could be stationed in and the lifelong friends she would make. She wasn't sure she wanted to join the Army, especially after meeting Larry but it sounded interesting, she would meet them and listen, but she wouldn't sign anything.

She told them she was busy until April, but she would stop by then and talk to someone, there was a recruitment center in Dorsey; she could walk there. She still had to walk everywhere or take the bus; she had taken a road test for her driver's license, but she failed! She couldn't seem to master the parallel parking; she would have to try again in June after school and graduation was finished.

Aunt China didn't have a license either, Nene had just gotten a license recently, but she never drove anywhere.

It seemed the Bobson women never drove, the men always drove, even with her license Nene walked everywhere or got people to drive her. It could be because Granpa always had the car and he was always working or at the lodge but even when the car was there, she did not drive it.

It was Saturday and Dina came to the house at 8:00 am so they could take a 10:00 am bus to Phila. They were going to Phila to get their gowns! Nene said they should eat breakfast first and they had pancakes and sausage. Everybody was eating breakfast, Nene, Aunt China, Renee and her brothers and Dina, Nene made pancakes from scratch and she even used a meat grinder to make her own special sausage. Breakfast was delicious and filling and it was finally time to walk into town to take the bus to go shop for gowns.

They walked to the bus depot and took the 10:00 am bus, it was March, and it was a windy day; thank goodness they had afros. The wind didn't affect their hair much.

They put on heavy jackets and gloves, but they refused to put on hats, they didn't want to mess up their hair; they wanted their hair to look nice as they tried on prom gowns.

It was 9:15 am, they had to take a 10:15 bus and Renee wanted to check the rainbow shop first to see if they still had the pink gown, she loved that gown; they could go into the city to look for Dina's gown.

They went into Rainbow and the gown was gone! Renee was crestfallen but Aunt China assured her they would find her a gorgeous gown in the city. They talked about Aunt China's prom gown and Dina's sister's gown and how beautiful they were. They talked about Prom decorations and dances and music back in the late 1960s when Aunt China had her prom. They talked about the boys who took them and the food they ate and other people at the bus stop started talking about their proms! Everybody at the bus stop talked about where their prom was and how memorable it was.

They said the prom and graduation was one of the most magical moments in life for a young person. They waited for the bus and dreamed of finding the perfect gown.

The bus ride to Philadelphia always took an hour, it seemed like it stopped at every corner; the view of houses and stores and people walking was interesting, but it was exasperating when the bus made so many stops.

They looked at the people who boarded the bus, some looked like housewives dressed in A-line dresses, matching spring coats and high heels, some looked like students with Afros and leather jackets. There was a mixture of people on the bus, were they going to the store, to a sports event or were they going to work?

The bus stopped and it was time for Renee, Aunt China and Dina to get off, it looked like they were in the center of Philadelphia. They started to walk, and Renee saw a street sign which read Market Street.

They noticed a big crowd of people a block away and Aunt China explained it was the fish market, people bought fresh fish and brought it home to cook. Nene didn't get her fish from a fish market, Granpa had a boat and he and his friends would go out on the boat and catch fish, they always had fresh fish and Nene's fried fish was delicious.

They saw no need to go to the fish market and they kept walking. They came upon a huge store called Strawbridge and Clothier, they went inside, and they sold food and small items; there was an elevator and moving stairs called escalators to get to the 3rd floor where evening dresses were. Renee and Dina had never seen a store this size, but Aunt China said the factory where she works makes clothes for stores like this, that is how she was able to bring clothes with minor defects home at a cheap price.

They went to the third floor and walked into a wonderland of formal evening gowns.

There were evening dresses which came right below the knees, there were A-lined dresses made of silk and satin; there were poufy dresses made of crinoline and lace, Renee had never seen so many dresses.

She noticed there were no other black people in the store, but the personnel seemed very friendly, they seemed ready to help at a moment's notice; one man followed them through every aisle.

They didn't need any help; they didn't ask the man for anything; this store was serious about customer service.

They walked into another room and there were rows of prom dresses of all fabrics and colors, they would probably be in this shop for hours!

They walked up and down aisles and Renee and Dina saw beautiful gowns, but they didn't see any they really loved, they were not the gowns they wanted to wear to the prom. Now a lady was following them through every aisle, this store really did have people ready to help.

Finally, they came to prom gowns in the middle of the store which were marked for Junior Misses, they were pretty, but they were not what Renee was looking for, however one gown caught Dina's eye.

It was a sky-blue gown with a sweetheart neckline, it came down past the ankles and it had a big blue sash around the waist, it was satin covered in a material which looked like feathers; it was beautiful, and it looked like it would cling to every curve. Dina loved it and she went to try it on, she was sure it would look great, Renee and Aunt China thought it would look great too.

Dina came out of the dressing room to show off the gown and they were all correct, she looked amazing! The gown flowed down past her ankles, it accentuated her small waist and hugged every curve; they all imagined blue high heels with the gown. The gown was $39.99, and she could get the blue heels for $15.99, she was ecstatic she had her prom gown, and she could get the blue heels she saw.

They looked for the lady who was following them to ask for help and she was nowhere to be seen, Aunt China said people following them weren't ready to help, they were making sure they weren't stealing. When Dina and Renee asked why they weren't following white people Aunt China said, that's the way it is.

Renee didn't see a gown comparable to the pink gown she saw when she went shopping with Aunt China before, she figured she would have to pick something, but she didn't see anything she liked.

They went to look at shoes and they didn't see anyone following them however there was a man a few aisles over in the lady's shoe department who seemed suspicious to Renee, he kept looking at them.

Dina finally found a pair of powder blue heels with a strap in the back which would go perfectly with the gown. Aunt China said it was lucky she didn't have to dye a pair of white shoes; it was hard to find the exact color.

CHAPTER 25
Renee Finds Her Prom Gown

Why did people keep following them around through the store?

Dina was satisfied, she had her gown and shoes, now they had to find Renee's gown and shoes. She went to the cashier to pay for her gown and shoes and the man who was looking at them disappeared. They looked around a little longer, but they saw they were not going to find anything for Renee.

Dina bought her gown and shoes, and they exited the store. Dina felt like a society lady with her Strawbridge and Clothier bag, this was one of the most exciting days of her life; she couldn't wait to show her mother. They had spent two hours in that store. It was now 2:00 p.m.

They were hungry when they left Strawbridge and Clothier and they stopped at a street vendor to get hotdogs and soft pretzels. They sat on a bench and they ate and talked before they continued to walk to find another store. They asked Aunt China if they would be followed in every store and she said they probably would. She said they should ignore it; some people were ignorant; they shouldn't let it spoil their day.

They passed stores but the window dressings didn't draw them in. It was a great day but being followed put a damper on it. Renee wondered if she were followed in stores in Dorsey, she never noticed but she would start to pay attention.

They had walked for quite some time when they arrived at a store called Gimbels. This was a huge store, it looked like it had many floors but not as many as Strawbridge and Clothier, it was similar with different goods on different floors, yet it was different. There seemed to be more small things on the floor, more toys, more tools, more Knick knacks. There were floors with TVs, radios and stereos, floors with hair salons, men's shops, children shops, linens, sewing machines; this store seemed to have more of a variety.

They thought this store was smaller, but it still had seven floors. They got on the elevator and went to the third floor where the evening wear was. They arrived at the third floor and it was a similar set up to the previous store. There was a man who followed them as soon as they started looking around. Aunt China told him they didn't need help. He moved back a few aisles, but he was still there.

There were rows of dresses and a room which led to formal evening wear. There were rows and rows of gowns just like the last store, they were very pretty but not what Renee was looking for. They even found the exact same gown Dina had just bought from the other store and it was the same price. Renee was going to grab one of the gowns so she would have something to wear at the prom when she glanced over to a row of gowns for Junior Misses on the side of the store. She walked over and saw more pretty gowns and she was disappointed until suddenly she saw her gown! It was the pink satin A-line gown with a scoop neck and a pink satin sash, it came down to the floor and would only show the front of her heels; she was delighted. Aunt China and

Dina were pushing her into the dressing room to try the gown on. She went into the dressing room and slipped off her blouse and skirt and she tried on the gown.

It was A-line, but it still flowed and swirled and clung to curves she didn't know she had. The scoop neckline accentuated her cleavage, and the sash highlighted her tiny waist. The gown came down to the floor she could only see the top of her feet. She walked out of the dressing room and Aunt China and Dina gasped. She looked so beautiful, they told her she had to get that dress. They didn't have to say it twice, she had every intention of getting this dress; she dreamed of this dress since she saw it in Dorsey, she couldn't believe it was the same price.

She hoped she could find matching shoes, she remembered Aunt China saying sometimes you had to dye shoes to get the perfect color to match your gown.

They went to the shoe department and much to Renee's delight, she found pink sling back heels which were the same color as her gown. Aunt China and Dina agreed they were perfect, and they were ready to purchase the items and head back home. They purchased the items and went downstairs to exit the store when they noticed a jewelry counter, most of the jewelry was much too expensive however they did see beautiful costume jewelry that was reasonably priced. There was a woman in the jewelry department who followed them, Renee wondered why, it wasn't expensive jewelry and why didn't they follow anyone else?

They saw a pink pearl necklace and matching earrings; it was a double strand and Aunt China said it would be a little longer than a choker; it would accentuate the scoop neckline and the pink pearl earrings would add the final touch.

Dina saw a gold pendant necklace with matching dangling gold earrings, she said it would really look good with her sky-blue gown and Renee and Aunt China agreed.

Both sets cost $10, Dina had added allowance money to her Halloween money, but she was still $2.00 short; Aunt China gave her the money as a prom gift.

They purchased the jewelry, and they were now ready to catch the bus. It had been a long day and they were eager to get back home with their prom treasures. They were also weary of people who followed them in department stores all day.

Renee wondered if all people who were "different" were followed and treated so unkindly. There was a lady in Dorsey, everyone knew her, they would see her walking down the street when they took walks around the town. She was a nurse, and she was one of the smartest, funniest people Renee knew. Nene and Aunt China said she was a transvestite, Renee thought she was gorgeous and classy; everyone liked her. Was she followed in stores because she was different?

Was the funny guy who dressed up in a police officer uniform to direct traffic followed? Everyone said he was crazy, was he treated unkindly? Renee didn't know, but she had a feeling the answer was, they were all treated differently. This put a damper on the day, they were happy it was time to leave.

They walked down the street with their bags, Aunt China helped carry some of the bags and they talked about the prom during the entire bus ride home. Aunt China also talked about the people who followed them in all the stores. She said she was going to send a letter to the headquarters of the stores, she didn't know if it would make a difference but at least it would be on record.

They walked Dina home from the Dorsey bus stop, and Aunt China walked Renee home. Aunt China went home and assured her she would help her get ready on prom night.

The next day was Sunday when the entire family came to dinner, they usually had dinner around 5:00 p.m. and Nene was finished cooking at Noon. She had a few hours before dinner, and she thought she would go visit her friend Mary. Nene had quite a few friends with whom she liked to have cocktails.

Among her cocktail friends was Dottie who was a tall brown, quiet stately woman in her late 40s, there was Grace a plump white woman who was loud like Nene, and there was Annie who was tall, brown and quiet, she kept a messy house.

Annie was one of Nene's best friends, but she didn't like to go to her house, Nene was very neat; she didn't care for messy houses. Nene and her best friend Annie could talk about anything over cocktails at Nene's house they could talk about other friends, children and husbands. It seemed all her friends had husbands who worked hard and were not around much, they had a lot to talk about.

Nene's friend Mary was her second-best friend, they could talk about anything and they loved cocktails together.

Mary was a plump, brown skinned woman with black luxurious hair, she went to the hairdresser every week. Mary's house was immaculate, and Nene loved going there, she was wonderfully comfortable in Mary's house.

The only problem Nene had with Mary was her parrot Larry. Mary had Larry the parrot since he was a baby, and he could really talk. Sometimes Nene would go to Mary's house and after Mary said Hi Bea, Larry the parrot would say "there she is loudmouth

Bea, squawk!" Nene did not like that parrot! She figured Mary talked about her, and Bea admitted she could be loud, but she did not like that parrot!

Nene was going to go see Mary before Sunday dinner and Renee asked if she could tag along, Renee loved going to Ms. Mary's house, she adored Larry the parrot. She loved to hear him talk and she got a kick out of him squawking about loudmouth Bea. Nene and Renee realized both Larry the parrot and Renee's new boyfriend Larry had the same name. Nene laughed and said thank goodness Larry the boyfriend had better manners than Larry the parrot!

Nene said she could tag along to Ms. Mary's, but Larry was not at her house anymore. Renee asked why on earth not. She knew how much Ms. Mary loved that parrot. She would never give him away. She knew he was old, probably around twenty, and she asked Nene if he died from old age. Nene said no, and she told Renee to sit down, and she recounted the story of what happened to Larry the parrot.

CHAPTER 26
Where Was Larry the Parrot? (Not Larry the Boyfriend)

Renee visits Army recruiter.

Nene had gone to Ms. Mary's house a couple of weeks ago and she noticed Larry the parrot wasn't there, even his cage was gone. She asked her what happened to him and Ms. Mary told her the story.

Larry was quite contrary one day during the previous week, he was squawking to the cat "get out cat!" *Squawk!* "Shut up, Bill!" (Ms. Mary's husband.)

For some reason he didn't want his favorite treat which were crackers. He kept squawking about "stupid crackers! Larry don't wanna cracker!"

Ms. Mary opened the cage door a tiny crack to get Larry and clean out his cage when suddenly, he flew out! The window was open, and he flew right out the window.

Ms. Mary was screaming no Larry, come back but Larry flew around and then landed and Ms. Mary tried to catch him to bring him back in the house.

Larry looked over his shoulder and saw Ms. Mary walking to catch him and he said, "shut up, Mary! *Squawk!* over his shoulder.

Larry was crossing the street still squawking shut up Mary while looking over his shoulder when a car hit him! He didn't see the car coming because he was looking behind him and squawking at Ms. Mary. She said all she saw was white feathers, they flew up and floated all over the street. That was the last of Larry, the beautiful white cockatoo parrot, she was despondent and crushed but she said it was devastating and comical at the same time. The last thing he did was looked over his shoulder to say, "Shut up, Mary!" *Squawk!*

Nene understood Mary's sadness. She didn't care for Larry, but she knew how much it hurt Mary.

She had to admit she thought Larry saying shut up Mary over his shoulder and feather's flying was sad yet kind of funny.

Renee decided she didn't want to go with Nene to Ms. Mary's, she only liked Ms. Mary's house because Larry was so lively and funny. She would be sad to go to the house and not see Larry, he seemed to be the life of that house. The cat was always somewhere sleep and the dog was normally outside.

She told Nene she would stay home but she asked her to tell Ms. Mary how sorry she was. It was going to be a different house without Larry, it would be sadder and quieter.

Nene went to Ms. Mary's house and stayed a few hours, when she got back, she was in a good mood and poured herself a cocktail why while she set the table for Sunday dinner.

The food was already cooked, all she had to do was heat it up and serve it. Of course, the family loved the Sunday dinner, there was always good food and great conversation.

After Dinner, the family even asked about Ms. Mary and how she was doing with the loss of Larry the parrot, everybody knew Larry the parrot. When Nene talked about him there was a moment of sadness, but it was followed by smiles when she recounted the story of Larry looking over his shoulders saying, "shut up Mary."

There were parakeets in the Bobson house, but they didn't talk, they were kind of boring compared to Larry the Parrot. The Bobson's had their share of pets, there were cats, dogs and fish tanks which lined the walls, Nene cleaned the tanks every week, it was quite a task. There were algae eating fish, but she still had to clean the tanks weekly. She would clean out the pumps and fixtures, she replaced the water and cleaned the entire tanks monthly.

The tanks were beautiful, there were huge angel fish in one tank, there were betas in another tank and tropical fish in another tank. There were two parakeets, a Siamese cat and of course Jose the dog.

Renee and her brothers weren't required to clean up after the animals except to clean the cat litter. The dog went outside by himself, Nene cleaned after the fish and birds.

Pets really did make a difference in a household, Renee didn't even like it when a fish died. She didn't want to think of one of the parakeets or the cat or the dog dying. She couldn't imagine the house without the rows of fish tanks, it made the living room look alive and exotic. She couldn't imagine the house without the cat who swiped at everybody or the dog who chased the kids around whenever they were in the house. Pets added life to the household.

Dinner was over, everyone went home, and Renee went upstairs to her room to watch TV. She was interrupted by a phone call from Larry the new boyfriend Prom date, it was a good day.

The next day was a normal school day and Renee decided to stop by the Army Recruitment office, she was going to wait until April, but April was a month away and she was excited to hear the information.

She walked into the office which had four desks. There was a recruiter at each desk. There were Army posters on all the walls and a huge American flag.

She had talked to a John on the phone, and she noticed him sitting behind a gold name plate at the second desk. She introduced herself and he told her to have a seat; he was smiling, jovial, and charming.

He told her about the Army: she would go to basic training to get into tip top shape, she would learn to use weapons and then she would go to training to learn about a specialty. She would take a test to decide which specialty would best suit her and she would be trained in that specialty. For instance, if the test showed she had a proclivity for engineering she would be trained in that.

If she scored high in math she might be in personnel or bookkeeping; if she scored high in English she might go into administration.

There were schools for all occupations or MOS (military occupational specialties).

Renee asked what about stories she heard of women having forty roommates in a big room. John assured her that was only for ten weeks and then it was on to occupational training and permanent duty which would mean one roommate, like college. He assured her she would meet lifelong friends; he was still friends with people he served with ten years ago.

The Army sounded cool to Renee, she could travel the world, she could meet new friends and she would be armed in case she ran into trouble. She decided to take the Army test or the (ASVAB, Armed Services Vocational Aptitude Battery) John said she could always back out of pre-enlistment even if she took the test. She scheduled the test for the end of June after graduation.

She told Nene and Aunt China about the Army recruiter, it would be respectable, she would have a salary with benefits, she could travel, and she would get education and housing after service.

They were not thrilled, they said she should go to college and she said she probably would. She didn't even need to think about the test until after graduation.

She had a good GPA for her last year of school, she had gotten a B in Math and Science and she had gotten A's in English, Spanish and History; she did better in communication subjects.

The school was buzzing with graduation and prom plans. She didn't talk much about Larry and her prom plans even though she saw him every weekend when she went to the clubs where he performed.

Dad wasn't always at clubs with Larry, sometimes he performed and laid tracks for his other group but sometimes he might sing lead or background vocals depending on the song.

She and Larry were getting serious, they would kiss and caress each other, and they spoke on the phone every night. They would sometimes go far, Larry would touch her all over and she was on fire, and for the first time it didn't feel wrong or weird.

She could imagine a life with him but not in Pennsylvania. She hoped he would change his mind and consider traveling, she wanted to see family on breaks, but she wanted distance. They talked about their dreams and accomplishments, Larry's dream was to make enough money singing, this way he would not need to work in a gas station or mechanic shop.

Renee talked about her dreams of travel and leaving small town life, it was the one thing she and Larry did not have in common. He seemed to like living in Pennsylvania, and he didn't have any intention of leaving, she hoped he would change his mind.

March turned into April and it was Easter, the temperature was in the mid-70s and the Easter church service was rather good. Renee and her brothers still got chocolate Easter bunnies and an excellent meal for dinner. Dad, Aunts, Uncles and Cousins were there; it was always a big family gathering. Larry had dinner with his large family for Easter, Renee did not see him that day, she was sorry he couldn't make it.

It was back to school the next day and everyone was still talking about the prom and graduation. Some teachers talked about how certain students with high GPAs and the best in the class would get an award at Graduation. Renee knew she had the highest grade in Spanish class, she wondered if she would get an award.

The Spanish teacher was not telling anyone who would get the award, she said there were a few candidates, it wasn't solely the grade but the extracurricular Spanish activities and other factors.

Renee participated in the Spanish tutoring program, and she had poems published in Spanish in the school newspaper, but she didn't know if other students did more. She would love to win that prize—it was $300! She didn't tell anyone about her hope of winning the Spanish award, she didn't want to get anybody's hopes up.

That night after school, Renee reminded Larry about her pink gown for the prom, he needed to wear something pink to match her gown; he assured her he would, and he would even bring her pink flowers.

The month of May was almost here, the last month was a whirlwind of activity, she and Dina and Fawn would walk around town and talk about the boys they were dating, they made plans to go to the town fair in May after the prom and they even watched the Muhammad Ali fight on TV at the end of April. He beat Jimmy Young, Howard Cosell acted surprised, and the girls loved it.

They loved Mohammad Ali, he was cute and confident, and he was also rich, and he traveled all over, he was the perfect guy.

Fawn had just started high school; she was not going to the prom, but her father was still taking her to sports events and Renee went to a couple of basketball games. She didn't tell Fawn or Dina about the Army yet; she wasn't sure she was really going to go, and she didn't want to tell them before she was sure.

For now, it was time to concentrate on the prom. Thoughts and planning for the prom were going to take up a lot of her energy for the next month.

She couldn't believe it was already May and it was prom day. Aunt China came over early to make sure everything was perfect. Nene made breakfast, Renee did her chores and then it was time to get her hair done.

Renee hated getting her hair done, it meant not wearing her afro. Aunt China would wash her hair, dry it and put grease on it to "straighten" it.

Straightening consisted of putting a hot comb made of steel on the fire, the hot comb was then used to comb through the hair to make the hair "straight." Aunt China was exceptionally good at straightening, she didn't burn her neck like Dad did when she was a baby. The problem was although Aunt China did not burn her with the straightening comb, the hot grease would drip on her neck and burn her, she hated it.

She did have to admit her hair was straight, glossy and thick when she finished, it made her look exotic. She had already taken her bath for the day and Nene and Aunt China said she could wash up when it was time to put on her gown, they did not want her to mess up her hair.

It was 4:00 p.m. and Aunt China told Renee to wash up and not to forget to wash her face good; a clean face is needed for make-up.

Aunt China started to apply the make-up. She put false nails on her fingers and polished them; they made her hands look nice. The nails were not super long, they looked quite pretty and natural, she also clipped and painted her toenails!

Next, she put on foundation and it hid her pimples! After the foundation came the eyeliner, eye shadow and mascara; the final touch was a rose-colored lipstick. Renee was not one to wear make-up, but she was glad Aunt China applied it, it looked perfect; her face was pretty!

Next Aunt China started on Renee's hair, it was thick, black and glossy from the straightening and now Aunt China put it up in a bun with curly tendrils which framed her face, Renee thought it was perfection. It had taken an hour to do the hair and make-up and Renee still had to put on the gown, heels and accessories; she started to wonder if she was going to be ready when Larry got to the house at 7:00 p.m.

Aunt China unzipped the dress and had her step into the gown, she did not want to pull the gown over her head. She zipped up the gown, and the scoop neck showed off just enough cleavage to be appealing yet acceptable. The gown clung to curves she didn't know she had, it flowed down to the floor accentuating her tiny waist; she slipped on her pink heels and only the toes and heels of the shoe were visible.

There was a wide silk band under the breast which circled her front and back, and there was a fabric bow on the back of the band which had material that streamed down the back of her gown to the bottom of the gown.

She was a vision in pink, Aunt China even entwined pink ribbon in her bun, she felt like a princess. Fawn was there and she squealed, she couldn't believe how great she looked.

She heard the doorbell ring, and it was Larry, she would be able to walk down the steps to the living room and make a grand entrance.

CHAPTER 27
It's Prom Night!

Aunt China and Fawn went downstairs first to announce her. Renee slowly floated downstairs and Larry looked pleasantly captivated, Dad was there, and Aunt China's husband Uncle Cark was there, even some of Nene's friends were there. Everyone applauded and looked at her with admiration, she loved the feeling, she was floating on air.

Larry told her how beautiful she looked and presented her with a wrist corsage of pink carnations to match her gown. He had on a black tux with a white shirt, a pink sash and a pink bow tie, he looked dashing. He had black pants and black, shiny leather shoes to complete his ensemble; they matched perfectly.

It was time to take pictures, everyone in the neighborhood wanted a picture of them on the lawn in front of the rose bushes.

There must have been fifty Polaroid pictures of Larry and Renee dressed for the prom in front of the rose bushes.

Renee was always worried about boys being shorter than her, she was 5'8" tall and most boys were her height or shorter, but Larry was taller than her even when she was wearing heels. They looked wonderful together in the pictures, Larry stood four inches taller than her in all the pictures. Their smiles were bright and genuine.

It was time to get into Larry's car, an Oldsmobile Cutlass and head off to the prom.

They got into the car and drove off. Renee liked Larry's car, it was roomy and always clean. It was shiny inside and out, the console sparkled, and it smelled like rich leather. She felt like a princess being escorted to the ball and she leaned back in her seat to take it all in.

They rode past the school, which was empty, everybody was probably getting ready for the prom or already there. They rode past Dorsey stores which were closing for the evening and they rode past houses, some people were taking prom pictures on lawns and some older people sat outside to enjoy the evening breeze.

Larry told her how pretty she looked, and Renee told him how great he looked. She asked him how he knew what color bow tie and sash to get, and he told her he knew when she described her gown. She described it as the color of Nene's pink roses, and it was a perfect description.

Renee asked him if he knew where the place was, it was the Hilton Hotel in Philadelphia, Larry said he looked at the prom tickets and got the address, he was surprisingly good with directions; they wouldn't get lost.

They were on the highway zooming towards Philadelphia and Renee remarked about the beautiful lights on the bridge they were about to cross. She had heard people talk about fear of riding over bridges, but it did not bother her. She loved the panoramic water view and the city off in the distance, she thought it would make a great painting or postcard.

Larry loved the view also, but he talked about one of his favorite bridges, the Chesapeake Bay Bridge in Virginia. He said it was one of the longest bridges he ever crossed, and it seemed to sway as you crossed it, the view was breathtaking.

He also talked about a bridge in New Orleans called the Lake Pontchartrain Bridge, he said it was a highway which seemed to cross the entire city. He said bridges don't normally bother him but that one seemed close to the water and it went on for miles. He didn't think the Lake Pontchartrain was as pretty, it looked like nothing, but water and it had only a few boats and hardly any landmarks. He much preferred this bridge in Philadelphia and the Chesapeake Bridge.

Larry was so knowledgeable about everything, it's one of the things she liked most about him, how can someone look so good and be so smart and nice? She couldn't believe her good luck in meeting him and going to the prom with him. It was hard to believe her first real boyfriend was so good looking, smart and charming.

Larry drove an hour, they talked about his band and his job, they talked about her school grades and her newspaper articles. They talked about the music they loved and the TV shows and movies they liked to watch and before they knew it, they were pulling up to the Hilton.

It was a grand hotel with blazing lights which lit up half of the block. The Parking Valet took the car to park it as they entered the ball room. There were huge chandeliers in the lobby and there was a booth to get your picture taken. Larry suggested they get their picture taken and they went beneath the archway for a photograph, the picture was a photo of a tall, thin, beautiful, smiling young couple who were out on the town, Renee would keep it forever.

They walked into the ballroom and it was magical, tables were covered with white linen table clothes, there was China, silverware and crystal for every place setting.

There was a band playing the latest hits from the 1970s, they mainly played mellow songs for the dinner hour. There were students decked out in gowns and tuxes at every table, everyone seemed to be ecstatic and friendly; they were friendlier here at the prom than they were at school.

Renee and Larry said hi to everyone they passed, they introduced her to their dates, and she introduced them to Larry. They told them they would see them later and they headed toward a table where Dina and her boyfriend Denny sat.

Both Dina and Denny looked spectacular, they looked like the perfect couple, they smiled and asked Larry and Renee to join them.

Dina was mesmerizing in her sky-blue gown and heels, she had on gold earrings, necklace and bracelet. She had blue combs in her hair which had been pressed and curled and cascaded down her back. Denny had on a sky-blue tux which matched Dina's gown.

He was Dina's height and he looked nice with his trimmed afro, but she thought he would look better in a black tux with blue trim. Renee thought Larry was probably the best-looking guy in the room, he even looked better than the band members!

Dina exclaimed with delight, she twirled Renee around and said she looked like a million dollars, she talked about how her, and Larry made a gorgeous couple, Renee and Larry glowed. She and Larry told Dina and Denny how great they looked, and they all took a picture.

The food was ok, it wasn't as good as Nene's food, but they all felt like adults dining on steak, green-beans and baked potatoes. The drinks were sparkling apple cider and Denny said somebody had spiked the punch.

Denny and Larry stood up, they wanted to see about the spiked punch, they asked the girls if they wanted some punch and Renee and Dina said "sure, why not."

Dina squealed with excitement, she pointed out all the girls and guys they knew, and she said none of them looked as good as they did. Renee laughed, when she looked around, she had to agree with her, they looked as good as anyone in the room, they even looked better than some people.

There were not a lot of black students in her class, Renee noticed there were only four or five other black couples out of hundreds of students, she wondered where the other black students were. There were probably about thirty or forty in her graduating class.

The guys came back with the spiked punch and Renee took a sip, it was strong, the drink spread warmth through her entire body, she felt giddy, confident and she was ready to dance.

They had all eaten their dinner and talked and now it was time to boogey. They were playing one of Renee's favorite songs, it was time to hit the dance floor.

The band played the opening beats to "Love Hangover" by Diana Ross and they sounded good; the female lead was electrifying. Everybody was on the floor dancing, before the song finished the band played "You Should Be Dancing" by the Bee Gees and everybody stayed on the dance floor. There was hardly anyone sitting down, everybody was shouting and dancing, they were getting quite a workout; the band really pleased the crowd.

Finally, Renee and Larry were about to head back to the table when the band started to play "Take it to the limit" by the Eagles, Renee and Larry decided to stay and slow dance. They glided to the mellow beat and smooth voices of the band, Larry held her tightly and guided her around the floor, it was marvelous. Renee looked around, everyone was still on the dance floor this was a good band and a magical night.

They went back to the table and had another glass of punch, they walked around and talked to people, they danced, and time seemed to fly. It was finally time to fill in ballots for prom queen and prom king. Renee nominated Dina for Prom queen and she nominated Terry her next-door neighbor as Prom King, she thought he was the best looking and most popular besides Larry. Terry was on the basketball team and he was a decent person; he came to the prom with his girlfriend Gina who was from Philly. Everyone turned in their ballots and waited for the winners to be announced.

It was already 10:30 and the prom ended at 11:00, Larry and Renee were slow dancing to "I write the songs" by Barry Manilow. At the end of the song, they started to head back to their table when the announcement was made about the prom queen and prom king winners. Renee told Dina she was sure she would win but Dina said there was stiff competition and Renee might win.

The announcer stated the committee counted all the ballots and the winner for Prom Queen was Renee! She couldn't believe it! She was in shock, she felt like she couldn't move, Larry and Dina pushed her up to the stage!

She couldn't think of anything to say, she thanked everyone for voting for her and she was given a sash and a gown! They then announced the prom king, and it was Terry from next door! Terry was one of the school's basketball stars but Renee was still shocked that he and she were picked out of everyone in the room. There were hardly any blacks in the room. They both received crowns and took a picture for the yearbook, they both looked shocked!

Renee went back to her table wearing her crown and sash and she was still in shock, but Larry, Dina and Denny were not shocked at all. Larry said she was the prettiest girl there and Dina said there was no competition with her gown.

Dina also reminded her how smart she was in school and how she was in the drama club and wrote for the school newspaper.

Renee was pleasantly surprised, she didn't think people really noticed her, she wondered if being Prom Queen required work?

It was 11:00 p.m. and the prom was ending, students were leaving; Dina and Denny were going to take a drive and go home. Renee didn't have to be home until 1:00AM, that gave her an extra hour to kill.

Larry asked if she wanted to see his apartment, it was only fifteen minutes from the hotel. Renee said sure; she would love to see where Larry lived.

They went outside and waited for the car. The parking valet drove it to the front of the hotel and Larry and Renee took off towards his house.

They talked about the prom and the music on the way to Larry's house, he thought the band was good, but he thought his band might have done some of the songs better; Renee agreed. They talked about Renee's surprise to being named Prom Queen and Larry said he would have been surprised if she wasn't prom queen.

Larry always made her feel special; she couldn't wait to see his house.

They pulled up to Larry's apartment building, it was a tall brick building; she wondered how many floors it had, and Larry said it had twenty floors!

They went into the lobby and there were metal boxes on the walls, Larry said they were mailboxes. The lobby was clean and bright, and Renee wondered who kept it so clean, there were no people to be seen. They got into an elevator and went to Larry's apartment which was on the twelfth floor! She couldn't imagine living so high up in the building, she wasn't afraid of heights, but she couldn't imagine living on the twelfth floor.

Larry's apartment door was right in the middle, apartment 1215. Renee asked him how he could afford to live on his own in such a place and he reminded her he was four years older than her; he was twenty-two. He was in a singing group, he was a mechanic and he worked at a gas station, he said he should be living in a bigger place, instead of a studio apartment.

They walked into the apartment and it was very neat, Renee laughed and said she was hoping it wasn't messy; Larry said never, he didn't like coming home to mess.

His studio apartment was one huge room, there was a kitchen and dinette set in one corner and a nice living room set on one side of the room. The living room set consisted of a deep brown leather couch and an overstuffed chair, there were also end tables and a coffee table.

There was a huge wardrobe and a chest of drawers in the corner near the couch for all his clothes and shoes. There was a bathroom off the main room with a nice tub, shower, sink, vanity and commode, everything was blue and black, it was nice, but she asked Larry where he slept? He explained how the overstuffed couch was a sleeping sofa, which turned into a bed. He described how he took it down at night and put it up in the morning.

He pulled the cushions off the couch and when he pushed down the bed was released; Renee had never seen anything like it before.

The bed already had sheets on it, the blankets and pillows were in the linen closet in the corner, this was a cozy, comfortable set up.

It was quite charming, Larry asked her if she wanted some Iced-Tea or Lemonade and she said she would take some lemonade.

They sat at the dinette set which was a glass table with four white chairs and they both sipped lemonades.

She told him how much she liked his place and he stated he liked it, but he was looking to get into a one bedroom which was roomier and had a separate bedroom. She noticed how quiet it was and he said his neighbors were quiet, he didn't really have any complaints, he was also quiet; he didn't practice his band music here in the apartment. His band did perform in the complex in the events room once and the people seemed to love it, he assumed that was the reason people accepted him. There were hundreds of tenants in his building and there were hardly any people of color there, he figured he was only one out of maybe five or six.

Renee could picture herself living in a place like this although she too would like a full bedroom.

 She told Larry how she had spoken to an Army recruiter and she pictured living like this after basic training if she decided to go into the military. Larry begged her not to go into the military, he told her he could at least visit her in school if she went to school in Pennsylvania and she said she probably would go to school; the army was just a pipe dream. He said good, he didn't want to lose her, and he leaned over for a kiss. It was a long deep kiss and both of their hands started to roam; Renee wondered what it would be like to go "all the way." This did not make her feel embarrassed or ashamed like the "late night visits" in the past. This felt natural and normal, she was excited, and she felt longing; she wanted to go to the next step.

Both her and Larry's breathing was heavy and labored, they couldn't keep their hands off each other and Renee was anxious to lose the virginity title.

She pulled Larry away from the dinette set and climbed onto his bed and said well, what now? He looked desperate and anguished when he answered.

He said they couldn't go any further, for one her Dad would kill him and for another it was almost 12:00 and they would barely make her 1:00 am curfew; Nene would never let him take her out again if they got home past curfew.

Renee was disappointed but she knew he was right, he took her face in his hands and said, "Don't get upset, we have plenty of time."

Larry, put the couch back up and they headed downstairs to get the car to start the long ride back to Dorsey. Larry sometimes held her hand while he was driving, she laughed and told him to keep his eyes on the road.

They finally arrived in Dorsey and parked in front of Renee's house, Larry kissed her good night and said he would call her tomorrow.

What a wonderful night, Renee couldn't wait to tell Nene and Aunt China about the prom, she wouldn't tell Nene about going to Larry's house; she would think it was inappropriate, but she would tell Aunt China and Dina. She couldn't wait to compare notes with Dina.

She took off her prom gown and hung it up, she washed off the makeup, took down her hair and put on her pajamas. She slept like a baby.

The next day she talked about the prom and Larry to Nene and Aunt China, she also told them how she was Prom Queen, and they were delighted. She told them how the picture was going to be in the yearbook and how Terry next door was prom king, she had to get a copy of her yearbook.

She ate breakfast and did her chores and went to find Dina, she was in front of her house; she didn't usually invite people in her house; Renee didn't know why; her house wasn't messy.

Renee told her about Larry's house and how they almost did it! Dina said her and Denny did it all the time. Renee asked how it was and Dina said it felt good, but it hurt at first.

Renee wanted to try it, but Dina made it sound like the initial pain was quite bad, it took away some of the anticipation. She figured Larry would be gentle, he said he would when it was time, but she didn't relish the pain of the first time.

Renee also talked to Aunt China about going to Larry's apartment after the prom and Aunt China wanted to hear every detail. It was funny, Aunt China didn't think it was shameful to have sex with a boy, she just thought it was shameful to make allegations against Granpa, but they never spoke of that.

Renee started to recount the visit to Larry's apartment after the prom. She told Aunt China what the building looked like and what the apartment looked like. She told her how he gave her lemonade, and they couldn't keep their hands off each other, but Larry said he didn't want to break curfew and he brought her home. Aunt China said Darn! Almost! She said maybe next time, and they both laughed.

Renee told her how one of her friends said it hurt the first time, and Aunt China said it hurt for a little while, then it felt good; they both laughed. Aunt China liked the idea of Renee having a boyfriend.

When Larry called that night, she asked about the pain of the first time and he said it was only for a minute and then she would like it. He told her not to worry about it, they had plenty of time and he would be gentle. He said she had nothing to worry about, they were crazy about each other and it would be great. They would be together for a long time; Renee loved this idea except she didn't like the idea of being together in Pennsylvania; she wanted to see the world.

The next day in school there was still talk about the prom and there was talk about Renee being Prom Queen, she had more pictures taken for the yearbook before the basketball game with Terry the prom king. People treated her differently, they asked her how Larry was, and they congratulated her on being Prom Queen.

CHAPTER 28
Last Year of High School

College? Exciting job? Military? Would Mom come to graduation?

She really liked her senior year of high school, now students were talking about graduation. The only difference between her and other students was her desire to get out of Pennsylvania after graduation. It seemed everyone else wanted to stay, they didn't even talk about leaving Dorsey.

A few students talked about going to college and Renee talked about being accepted for admissions to Penn State. Everyone was thrilled about being accepted to college, but no one was going out of state. They got offers to Pennsylvania colleges such as Cheyney and Swarthmore, but they didn't get offers for out of state colleges, she wondered if they applied.

She applied for out of state colleges, and she got acceptance letters from NYU and SUNY, but she didn't know if she wanted to go there either. She thought they might be good, but she really wanted to see the world, she didn't think NY was really the world. She would probably decide after graduation; she would let colleges know which one she chose in July, Nene suggested Penn State and Aunt China suggested NYU.

Dad and Larry were also fans of Penn State, Dad liked it because it wasn't far from home and Larry liked it because he could visit often. He figured they could really be a couple once she was out of Nene's house.

Larry figured he would be in a famous singing group and Renee would go to school for Social Work and probably be a famous psychiatrist. He told Renee their future was set.

Dad and Aunt China took her on tours of the Pennsylvania Universities, they were idyllic with rolling hills and collegiate buildings, students were rushing to class.

There were welcome tours and discussions of student activities and it was all quite exciting.

Dad and Aunt China were thrilled and so was Renee, but she couldn't stop thinking about the rest of the world. She dreamed of other states and other countries. She wondered how other people lived.

The talk at home and school was the High school graduation. There was talk in classes about students with high GPAs who might receive awards at the graduation and there was talk of purchasing caps and gowns and graduation pictures.

Renee received her final grades and was approved for graduation; she had a B+ average and she was ready to graduate. She had made it through high school!

There was a whirlwind of activity, she purchased her cap and gown and took pictures, one picture was with the cap and gown and one picture was a dress picture with a black silk shoulder drape, she wore pearl earrings and a pearl necklace for both pictures. She hoped the pictures turned out nice, she imagined

Nene would put them in the living room like she did with Aunt China's graduation picture.

The graduating class was small, only two hundred students; they were each given ten tickets. Nene said there would be enough tickets for her and Granpa, Aunt China, Uncle Carl, Renee's brothers, Nene's sister Aunt Sadie, along with her husband Uncle Willy and their Sons Arthur and Darius. She asked if Mom would be coming, they had not gotten an answer, she didn't get an answer when she asked either. She said she wanted to invite Larry and Aunt China said maybe Uncle Carl could stay home. Renee said she would call the office to get another ticket and the office gave her eleven tickets. She was relieved, she didn't want to leave Larry out.

Aunt China asked Renee if she was going to get the class ring and she told her no, she didn't really want the class ring; it looked big and bulky to her. She thought it was too much money for something she would probably never wear.

She would probably not wear the cap and gown again but at least it would take a nice picture in the yearbook and it would look nice hanging in the living room.

It was the day before graduation and it was finally becoming real, the class practiced lining up in the auditorium behind the stage in alphabetical order, they practiced walking across the stage to get the diploma and shaking the hand of the school board President.

There was a run through of speakers, award presentations and standing and seating assignments; they were ready for the next day's graduation ceremony.

The next day Renee got up and put on a nice dress with short heels and her lucky pearl earrings and necklace; she looked like a respectable young lady. Aunt China had straightened and hot curled her hair for this special occasion and with the addition of the cap and gown and pearls she looked like she was ready to conquer the world.

She had to leave an hour early for the last practice and Nene said the family would be there in plenty of time to cheer her on.

She walked up the street to the school and went to the auditorium where students were lining up. It was 12:00 p.m., an hour before the ceremony.

Her last name began with a B which meant she was at the beginning of the line, they practiced once more for the last time.

They lined up to get ready for their march down the aisle to the song pomp and circumstances where they would all sit in the front row in the same order. It took them almost an hour to get ready for the march, but they were now ready.

Everyone acted serious and focused for their big entrances, they were determined to impress all the guest.

They all marched down the auditorium aisles and the guest were already seated, Renee glanced over at the guest in the audience, and she saw Larry and her family; they were yelling her name as she marched down the aisle with her class.

They marched to the front rows and were seated alphabetically, they now listened to all the guest speakers. The guest speakers included the mayor, school board members, the Principal, teachers and the class valedictorian.

The valedictorian spoke first, Renee had a couple of classes with her, she had an A average, and she was in a lot of clubs; she would probably get most of the awards.

After the valedictorian spoke, the mayor, school board members and principal spoke, it was a warm, bright sunny day, and the auditorium was hot even with the fans; they had already been there an hour.

The principal went up to the podium and began to call students up to the stage to receive their diploma and shake hands. Renee went up when her name was called and went back to her seat. When all their names were called, they moved the tassels on their caps from the right to the left because they were now graduates!

It was now time for the teachers to speak and it was already 2:00 p.m., now they would present awards to outstanding students in their classes. The basketball and football coaches presented MVP awards to the outstanding athletes, Terry from next door got an award for basketball, students and guest clapped and whistled.

Jerry got an award from the Band Director for outstanding service and leadership for the marching band and the crowd again clapped and whistled enthusiastically.

There were awards for club participation and academic achievements awards for different subjects, all received enthusiastic clapping from students and audience.

Renee felt a sense of fellowship and pride, but the service was already an hour and a half, how long was this service going to last? She was surprised the guest didn't start leaving. There were so many teachers giving out awards she thought they would be there forever. Suddenly her Spanish teacher got up to announce the award for the student who showed Academic excellence and community service in the Spanish Department. The Spanish teacher called Renee's name! She couldn't believe it, she thought for sure the valedictorian would get the award, Renee had a high GPA in the class, and she was in a Spanish club, but she still didn't seriously think she would get it, students started nudging her to get out of her seat to get the award!

She got out of her seat to go to the stage to get the award and she knew she would need to say a few words. She couldn't think of anything to say! How did anyone who won an award come up with something to say so quickly? She got up to the stage, accepted the award from the Spanish teacher and thanked her. She then went up to the microphone and said Gracias a todas las invitadas y functionaries de la escuela or thank you to all guest and school officials.

She thanked the school for the opportunity to grow and learn different languages and cultures, she assured them it would be a memory she would never forget. She thanked the Spanish teacher once again and went back to her seat. The Spanish teacher beamed, and the audience cheered and whistled, she could hear Larry and her family cheering the loudest; it was a proud moment.

There was still a half hour more of the graduation ceremony and finally the principal congratulated all the award winners, thanked all students and family and wished everyone a successful and prosperous future. It was 4:00 p.m., the ceremony ended up being three hours long!

The class stood up and each student went to find their guest and go outside. Renee went outside with Larry and her family to take pictures with a Polaroid camera, everyone was smiling and taking pictures with the graduate.

Dina came over to take pictures and Fawn came over to congratulate her, her cousin graduated, and she slipped away from her family to take a picture with Renee.

After the picture taking and the meetings with friends and schoolmates Nene told Renee the family was going to treat her to dinner at Dorsey's steak house, it was one of the finest restaurants in Dorsey and they had delicious steaks and lobster.

She wondered why her mother's side of the family were not involved with her graduation day; they were involved with other cousins. Renee did not understand it.

Renee couldn't worry about it, she and her family went to the steak house, it was expensive; this was truly a special occasion.

They all got in separate cars and rode to the steak house; Renee and her brothers rode with Larry.

It was only a short ride to the steak house, but it was long enough to mention how long the graduation ceremony was.

The reservations were already made, and the tables were set up in a separate room. There were two long tables in the center of the room with booths around the perimeter of the restaurant. The tables had white linen tablecloths, crystal, fancy silverware and China; much like the prom settings.

Renee Larry and her family went to the tables which were pushed together, it fit eleven of them very comfortably.

They looked at the menu, Renee and Larry ordered steak and lobster, she was going to order a burger, but they told her to splurge, it was already paid for.

They asked her what she loved to eat more than anything and she laughed and said Nene's fried chicken. Everyone agreed but they said she couldn't get that here, they asked what the second thing was. The second thing was Surf N Turf or steak and lobster, she only had it once and it was delicious, but it was so expensive! They told her not to worry about the cost and she ordered it.

It was 5:00 p.m. and everyone was hungry. They all ordered their favorite meal from the menu. Some had pork chops, some had steak, some had fish. The waiter brought them rolls and butter for the table and they all dug in while waiting for their entrees.

Everybody at the table told Renee how excited they were for her; she was a graduate now and she won the Spanish award! Her cousin's Arthur and Darius told her how they yelled her name when she got the award and she laughed and said she heard them, she thanked them for being there for her.

The entire family congratulated her on the Spanish Award. Nene and Aunt China told her they always knew how smart she was, Granpa congratulated her and said he knew she was going to be successful, and Larry complimented and praised her for her accomplishment. She felt like she was the most successful girl in Dorsey.

Dinner still had not arrived, so the conversation turned to plans Renee had for her future, was she going to college? Was she going to work? She said she had a few offers from colleges, Penn State and Cheyney among others, she was considering all of them.

She let them know she also was considering the military, she wanted to travel around the world and see different countries.

Granpa and Uncle Willie had been in the military and they said it might be ok for a couple of years but they both thought college would be better.

Larry, her brothers, Nene and Aunt China thought college and a good job afterwards would be the way to go. Her cousins thought the military and traveling around the world sounded exciting, they thought it sounded better than college and a regular job in Pennsylvania.

She told them she was going to take the military test at the end of June, and she would decide after seeing her test scores which would determine which job she would get in the military. She certainly didn't want to be a chef or an engineer in the military, she would decide after the test.

She didn't think NYU was a real change from Pennsylvania, but she thought it might be an interesting atmosphere. Larry laughed and said he would get to visit a college girl; he would love it, and everyone laughed and looked around to see if they could see their waiter with their dinner.

As soon as they started looking for the waiter a bunch of waiters came out of the kitchen with rolling carts topped with big, covered silver trays, there must have been six waiters. When they came to the table, they uncovered the silver trays and uncovered different meats, vegetables and seafood. The food was sizzling as if it just came from the stove. They uncovered the last dish and there was a sizzling steak with a separate dish for lobster tails, it was finally time to dig in; everyone was famished.

The steak melted in Renee's mouth and the lobster dipped in butter was scrumptious, she couldn't remember the last time she tasted anything so delicious. Everyone at the table raved about the food, it was so delicious all you could hear was people eating and grunting with satisfaction.

They were at the restaurant for three hours but unlike the graduation. Three hours flew by. They finished their dinner and went back home, although the night was not over yet, there was still a graduation dance at the lodge at 8:00 p.m., everyone in the family was going including Larry.

Renee had to get home and take off her cap and gown; they wanted her to wear it at the restaurant, but she was now ready to take it off. She was already ready for the dance, she had on her nice dress and heels under the graduation gown, she was ready to party.

The entire family freshened up and drove to the lodge for the Graduation dance. The lodge was decorated with the school colors of blue and white. There were blue and white flowers along the walls and each table had a white tablecloth with blue flowers. There were blue and white streamers and graduation signs and banners.

CHAPTER 29
Graduation Dance, Last Dance

Is Larry backing away? More military information.

The room was dimly lit, the music was already playing, and the dancers were spinning and twirling on the dance floor. There was a mixture of people in the Lodge Hall, there were students and their families which included younger brothers and sisters and grandparents.

This was the first time Renee noticed there were no white people at the lodge, she wondered where the white graduates went for dances and parties.

The people at the dance were all different ages but everyone was on the dance floor. The music included top hits of the day, such as "Car Wash" from Rolls Royce and hits from the 1950s and 1960s such as "Mona Lisa" by Nat King Cole, "My Girl" by the Temptations, and "Respect" by Aretha Franklin.

It was a joyous occasion, and everyone was celebrating, Renee, Larry, and her brothers were on the dance floor dancing to Superstition by Stevie Wonder. Little Roy and Larry were doing the robot, and everybody was clapping and laughing. Finally, the song went off and Just to Be close To You by The Commodores came on, Larry and Renee got to slow dance, slow dancing was always magical with Larry. They would step and sway to the music and Larry would twirl her around, it was always a showstopper.

Midnight came in no time; it was the end of the graduation dance and it was time to go home. Larry drove her and her brothers' home and drove off after saying good night, Renee and her brothers went into the house singing. Nene was already home, she told Renee there were graduation cards and gifts she needed to open but it could wait until the morning; they were all tired now.

Renee agreed, she couldn't wait to get out of those clothes and wash up and go to bed; she was exhausted. Everyone went upstairs, washed up and went to bed, they were all bone-tired from the day's celebrations.

The next day was Saturday and Renee and her brothers went down to breakfast, Reggie Jr and Little Roy had jobs as bag boys at the local supermarket; they went to work after breakfast. Renee had a babysitting job in the afternoon, but she would do her chores first and babysit in the afternoon, after babysitting she was going to go to watch Larry play at a club in Philadelphia.

Dad wasn't in the band Larry played with at this club. Nene was going to stay home, she said she wasn't feeling well and Granpa wasn't home, he didn't work Saturdays; he must have already gone to the lodge.

Nene went back to bed after breakfast, it was Renee's chore to wash the dishes and clean the kitchen; she wondered what her family would do when she went to college or the military.

She did her chores, babysat, and waited for Larry to pick her up to take her to the club where he was performing tonight. She noticed the club was near Larry's apartment at a big fancy hotel and the music was a mixture of soul and pop music, the crowd was older people, probably in their 30s and 40s. It was a cordial and entertaining event and Renee enjoyed the evening, but she didn't think it was as exciting as some of the other clubs.

During a break she asked Larry which band was more enjoyable and he said he liked them both, but he tended to like the crowd better when he played with Dad's band.

Larry asked her if she had given any more thought about College or the military and she told him she would probably choose college and they would get to see each other when she went away to school. She reminded him about the military test she would be taking next week but she probably wouldn't enlist unless they put her in some glamorous job she couldn't resist, she was sure that wasn't going to happen.

Larry dropped her off and promised to call her the next day, the last couple of days had been extremely busy and Renee gladly retired for the night.

Renee was ready to open her graduation gifts. It was a Monday. Granpa was at work and her brothers were at school. Renee and Nene opened all the graduation gifts, they had called Aunt China, but she couldn't get off work. She told them to call her after work to let her know what the gifts were.

Aunt China had given Renee beautiful outfits from the factory, she was a secretary now, but she still got amazing discounts.

There were designer suits with matching skirts and jackets, there were dresses and there were bell bottomed pants; she had six different outfits.

There was a birthstone, matching earrings, and necklace set from Nene and Granpa, it was a dainty yellow stone with crushed diamonds around the stone; it was beautiful. She told Nene it was too much; it must have cost a fortune! Nene said there was nothing too good for her girls, Renee and China would always have the best.

Renee then opened the cards, most were from relatives from out of town, each card had a check; when she counted the checks, it was over $1000! Nene told her to put the money in the bank and to put half in a government savings bond and that's exactly what she did. She knew she could get financial aid for college and if she decided to join the military, they would cover basic living expenses; she would be able to save her money.

It was nighttime and Renee was waiting for Larry's call, but he never called, she assumed he was busy that evening.

Larry didn't call for a few days and she finally called him, he said he was in another singing group and practice had been crazy; he worked, practiced, and fell into bed exhausted at night. He said he missed her and would see her this weekend, he would take her to see his new singing group.

She said okay. She loved Larry's voice and he could really play the keyboard she was sure he would be successful, she wondered why he didn't want to explore other states. No one she knew from Dorsey or even Pennsylvania wanted to explore other states or countries. Not Larry, Nene, Aunt China or any of her friends. She wondered if most people in the country were closely tied to their birthplace.

She reminded Larry about the military test tomorrow, he told her to let him know about the results.

She said she would let him know but it took a couple of weeks to get the results. He told her he was still hoping she would go to college instead of the military.

The next day she ate breakfast before taking the bus to Philadelphia. She talked with Nene and her brothers; they couldn't imagine her going into the military, but they figured it wouldn't hurt to take the test.

Renee walked to the bus terminal and wondered about the test, she wondered if it was going to be difficult, what if she didn't pass it? She knew it consisted of Math and English; she wasn't really worried about the English portion but what if she failed the Math portion? What kind of math would it be? Would there be long math word questions? She was so absorbed with these questions she hardly realized this was her bus stop. She yelled out to the driver, this was her stop and she needed to get off, she left the bus to walk the blocks to the Army test site, this could change her life.

She arrived at the site and checked into the Military Processing Center and waited. There were a lot of people there, most seemed to be her age, but most were guys, and most were white. There were a few people of color, but she thought that was because it was Philadelphia which had a large population of people of color.

She wasn't surprised to see there were not many girls there, she knew the military was not really a common female occupation. She looked around the room and started talking to guys who were next to her, she asked if any of them were as nervous as she was?

They said they certainly were, they heard it was a tough test; they were worried about the English portions. She told them she was worried about the Math portion, what if there were word problems?!

They were all finally called into the testing room, they were seated and given a copy of the written test, they would be told when it was time to start.

They were told to open their booklet and begin the test. Renee looked at the first question which was reading comprehension and she breezed through it, as a matter of fact she breezed through the entire English portion, she thought this really isn't that bad.

She was surprised at the science questions on the test, but she was sure she answered them correctly. She then started to answer math questions and although some were word problems, they were not that bad. She was beginning to think she might pass this test with ok grades.

She then came to a part of the test called assembling objects. She had to look at a picture of an unassembled box and determine what it would look like after it was assembled. She had to pick from four choices.

The first questions seemed simple to Renee. She only had to look at a picture with four separate pieces and decide what they would look like. They then became difficult; some of the questions wanted you to assemble boxes after providing ten or fifteen pieces per box. She couldn't imagine what the boxes would look like after they were assembled with the picture of the pieces provided. The answer could have been any of the boxes.

She was starting to get a massive headache and toward the end of the assembling objects portion she looked at the pictures with the pieces and started guessing. She figured if she couldn't pass this portion of the test maybe her scores in the English and Math would help her pass it.

The test was three hours long. She thought she would breeze through it when she answered the English, math, and science sections, but now she had to assemble objects from a picture, and she didn't know if three hours would be enough time.

She had already taken two and a half hours. She didn't think she could finish, but she was finally finished that portion and she only had to answer a few more English questions. She finished just in time, she left the building; she felt both dread and relief.

She looked for a store for some aspirin for her headache, that was one of the hardest tests she had ever taken. She certainly didn't find the college entrance exams or even the SATs this hard.

Even though she thought she would probably end up going to college she was the kind of girl that had to do her best in everything she did. She could not imagine doing poorly in a test, she would always give it her all. She would be proud no matter what she got in the military test; she had done her best. She walked to the bus stop and rode the bus back home to Dorsey; she was glad she took the test it would be a great talking point, but she would be sad if she failed it; she did not like failing things.

She walked into the house and her brothers were not there, but Nene was there having cocktails with her friends, she asked how the test went and Renee said it was tough and she didn't know if she passed. Nene said she was sure she passed; she was very smart, but she still thought she should go to college instead of the military. Renee thanked Nene for having faith in her ability, it made her feel better about her odds; Nene was very astute in most things.

Renee went upstairs to call her recruiter to ask about the length of time it took to get the results back, he said it was usually a few weeks.

She said it was hard and she didn't think she aced it, he said you really can't look at it as acing it; you either pass or fail and it looks at your strength in a subject to determine the best occupation.

He said she was very smart, and she probably passed, she would probably qualify for a great occupation or MOS (military occupational specialty).

She called Larry later that night and he said the same thing as Nene, he said she was smart and probably passed with flying colors, but he hoped she would go to college.

Everyone believed she passed the test except her but then again, they weren't there to see the questions.

CHAPTER 30
Is Larry Saying Goodbye?

A new beginning for Renee. Goodbye, Dorsey. Hello, world.

Renee went to see Larry perform with his new group on the weekend, but he was busy the next week, they rarely had time to talk. A week later she went outside to the mailbox to get the mail and she saw a big Manilla envelope with her name on it. Inside the envelope was another envelope with white labels on the front and back, they both said do not open, the envelope must be taken to the Army recruiter; you could call your recruiter if you had any questions.

She immediately called the recruiter and he told her she could stop by it was probably her test scores. Nene was at her friends' house and her brothers were at school, she had done her chores; the house was sparkling, and she decided she could walk to the recruiter's office to see her scores.

She arrived at the recruiter's office with the envelope, and he opened it and he started to explain the results.

He said the test determines strength in certain areas which could determine an occupational success. He told her she passed the test, and he would go over each section's results.

He explained her results in mechanical comprehension, Auto Shop, Electronics and Math, her scores in those areas were average. She asked what category were the boxes which had to be mentally assembled, and he said that was mechanical comprehension and she scored average.

He said her lowest score was Science, but she passed it. He said her top score was in Reading Comprehension and Word knowledge, she scored remarkably high.

She was not surprised about the English portion, but she was surprised at the mechanical comprehension. She was pleased she passed the test.

He explained how her test scores showed she would be successful in administration. She could be an executive secretary for a company commander or even a post commander. She could serve in the US or a foreign country.

She asked what the difference was in a company or post commander and he explained a company commander oversaw one company in a battalion. There were four platoons in a company and four squads in a platoon. A battalion commander oversaw six companies, the battalion commander oversaw more people than the company commander; a battalion was almost like a small city.

He explained she could also work in a personnel unit which handles paperwork for new recruits, she could work in a Military Intelligence Unit; she thought Military Intelligence in another country sounded exciting.

She asked about basic training and he said she had to be in good shape, there would be physical training which would include cardio exercises such as running, there would be strength exercises and there would be introduction to weapons firing, self-defense and military protocol.

It sounded glamorous to Renee, she could see herself in a nice crisp uniform as a secretary to a battalion commander or even an office of personnel secretaries. The idea of working in another country filled her with awe and excitement. She asked how she would learn to do the job of a secretary to a post commander or a secretary who works in personnel?

He told her after basic training there is a school called AIT (advanced individual training), the school would teach her skills needed to be a secretary for a commander or a personnel office or any other office in the military.

She told the recruiter she would come back with a decision by next week, she needed to speak to her family first.

On the walk home, she weighed her options; she could go to college in the Northeast and get a job in the Northeast or she could go in the Army, travel the world. She would learn self-defense and how to shoot rifles and throw grenades! On top of that her housing, healthcare and meals would be paid for plus she would get a check. It sounded great to her; her mind was practically made up already.

She went home to talk to Nene and by then her brothers were home, Nene tried to talk her into college, but Renee thought the Army was a better choice, her brothers thought it sounded exciting. Pretty soon Aunt China was there, Dad was there and Granpa was home from work, of course Mommy wasn't there.

Aunt China and Dad preferred college but Granpa said she would get to see a lot of the world. Granpa had been in WW2, he was in France, Italy, Germany and he said it was a unique experience which he would never forget. He reminded her it was the military and could be dangerous or even life threatening.

Renee thought life could be dangerous, there were college students killed on campus, kids killed in gangs and people killed in bar fights. She also reminded them there was no active war going on.

They decided she already sounded like she made up her mind and she was eighteen; she didn't need their permission. They resigned themselves to Renee going into the Army.

The next day Renee went to the recruiter to complete the paperwork, she was given a packet with papers called orders.

She was to report to a center in Phila to take a physical, repeat the oath and ship out to basic training. The orders said she would be shipping out in August!

There was a list of things she could bring, and it needed to be packed in a duffle bag. The list was for six weeks of basic training and she wondered if she could fit it all in a duffle bag. It included clothes, underwear, socks, shoes, toiletries; they didn't want her to bring much so hopefully she wouldn't have a problem packing.

Larry was busy practicing with his band, and he hadn't called her. She called Larry and told him she was going into the Army in August.

He said he would miss her, and she had better write him, but he would see her over the weekend.

She saw Larry that weekend and he told her he would be busy for the next few weeks, he had to go to NY and Boston with his band and he might not see her before she went into the Army, it was already July and she was leaving next month. She told him she would write him, and they hugged and kissed and said goodbye.

She felt sad about not seeing Larry, but she was still excited about her new life. She imagined she could make a lot of new friends in the Army. She was sad about not seeing Aunt China, her brothers and Nene and even Granpa but the excitement outweighed the sadness.

She went to the department store to get a duffle bag and she started cleaning out her room. There was not much to clean out, she left most of her clothes and shoes there and there was not much else to take with her.

The day before leaving she said goodbye to everyone, but they said they would drive her to the train station, she would be going to Ft. McClelland in Alabama for basic training.

The next day Granpa drove her to the train station, Nene and her brothers were in the car, while Dad, Aunt China and her husband Carl followed in another car. They rode and talked about Dorsey and they made Renee promise to call and write, she promised she would.

They all got to the train station and the train was already there, Renee hugged everyone and promised to call and write as soon as she could. She got on the train and waved goodbye to her family, Dad and the women were in tears, her brothers stood silently and waved goodbye.

Renee waved until she could no longer see them; she then settled back and wondered about the next exciting chapter of her life.

Goodbye Dorsey, goodbye Pennsylvania. She was ready for the Army and Fort McClellan Alabama; it was a new day and a new world. Surprisingly, she had no tears.

ABOUT THE BOOK

This semi-autobiography about Renee Bobson, a black woman, and her family and ancestors is set in the late 1950s; however the scenarios and events can be compared to the stories of her ancestors in the 1800s. It particularly details the life of her ancestor, Annie from Ireland, who experienced the horrific aftermath of the Civil War, the assassination of Lincoln, and the Great Chicago Fire—experiences that Renee find similar to hers, with a different set of characters and timeline. It is a story about family and events in time throughout the ages. This is the first book of the trilogy.

The first book includes unsavory subjects such as child molestation, infidelity, and racism from the point of view of the author—personal experiences she went through from age three to eighteen. Her story is too real and scandalous to write under her true name, which is why a pseudonym is used, Renee Bobson.

Book two will be about Renee's enlistment in the military as well as her ancestor's time in the military. It will include marriage, children, and divorce. Book three will be about the older Renee, or present time. Children have grown, and Renee works for the state.

These trilogy will be heartbreaking, hilarious, triumphant, and hopeful—as life usually is all those things. These stories can be told throughout time.

Perhaps the actions of present-day family members are connected to the actions of family members from the past who were slaves or indentured servants. Perhaps we all have similar stories with different characters. As the Bible states, "There is nothing new under the sun."

www.ingramcontent.com/pod-product-compliance
Lightning Source LLC
LaVergne TN
LVHW091532060526
838200LV00036B/580